We Choose to Thrive

Our Voices Rising in Unison to share Messages of Inspiration and Hope to Childhood Abuse and Domestic Abuse Survivors

Becky Norwood

Publisher: MBK Enterprises, LLC
Publication Date: 2017
©2017 by Becky B. Norwood All Rights Reserved
©2017 The Woman I Love. All Rights Reserved

ISBN-10:0-9971687-3-0
ISBN-13:978-0-9971687-3-0

Library of Congress Control Number: 2017900638

Edited by Jay Polmar – Speed Read America
Design, Layout and Graphics by: Becky Norwood
Cover Design by: Angie Ayala
Foreword by: Jane M. Powers

Contributing Authors: Jo Dibblee, Cheryl-Ann Webster, Traci Bogan, Karin Tyson, Nishea Martinez, Carmel de Bertaut, Shanna Maria, Janet J. Bentley, Deborah Kinisky, Heather Egan, Brenda Hammon, Edna J. White, Shannon Gardner, Diana Dunham-Young, Amanda Hollis-Thompson, Nikki Dubose, Michele Croswell, Shannon O'Leary, Karen Mason, Renee Jean, Tessa Milne, Roberta Brown, Terri Lanahan, Sylvia Goalen, Souraya Christine, Christina Wensell, Teresa Syms, Sondra Joyce, Kaelen Revense, Jane M. Powers

All rights reserved. No part of this book may be reproduced in any form, by any means including, but not limited to electronic, mechanical, or information storage and retrieval systems - except in the case of brief quotations embodied in critical reviews and articles – without written permission from the author.

This book is based on the real live personal experiences and opinions of each person interviewed and have been published with the permission of the interviewee. The author will not be held liable or responsible to any person or entity with respect to alleged damages caused directly or indirectly by the information within this book.

Contact: Becky Norwood thewomaniloveisme@gmail.com

Dedication

This book is dedicated to all victims of abuse. No matter what type of abuse nor the enormity or lack of enormity of the abuse, there is no measuring device that can determine how it has affected your life.

We have come together to join arms and hearts to briefly share our stories with you. Our purpose is to offer hope and inspiration for your own healing journey. It is to expose the hideous epidemic that is abuse, whether that came from early childhood, as a young adult or as an adult.

There is great power in forgiveness, but know that abuse survivors suffer greatly from shame, and as such forgiveness must be for yourself, first and foremost.

Our stories are written to shed light on the fact that healing can take place. To inspire that healing so that we can best serve our families, our communities and our world and BE the change our world so needs.

In these pages, you will read words like:

Be a Champion of Abuse, not a Survivor!
Stand ON Your Story not IN It!
Stand Up, Speak Up, Command Your Inner Power, Find Your Truth

and

Choose to Thrive!

We Have Made that Choice

Will YOU?

"I do this to be a voice, to speak for those who can't speak."

~ Matt Sandusky

Table of Contents

Foreword

By Jane M. Powers

The book you hold in your hands contains some of the most powerful stories about abuse you will ever experience. I've been profoundly touched and moved by the depth of each and every one. These are no ordinary stories that give you just the cold hard facts. They allow you to discover and understand the process of going from merely surviving to thriving. If you're reading *We Choose to Thrive,* then I'm guessing you have a story of survival or you know someone who does.

Becky Norwood takes the power of these stories and delivers them with meaning and purpose to change lives. Her book not only sheds light on the reality of sexual abuse and other abuses, but also creates a defining moment for you, the reader, to decide how you will live. Will you choose to merely survive or will you thrive?

For too long, the secret of abuse has shamed, silenced and destroyed the dreams of far too many people. Well, no more! It's time we find the voice of truth and empower others to do the same. These stories bring to light the grim truth about the countless lives affected by abuse. But make no mistake, this book is not a collection of tragic "war stories." *We Choose to Thrive* is a compilation of achievements, successes, and triumphs by women, myself included, that demonstrate how we defied the odds stacked against us.

I believe there is no better way to change lives than through the power of one's voice. No matter what you have experienced in life, sexual abuse or not, you must discover and find your voice. In finding your voice, you find your power. The freedom that comes from your own internal power will provide you the confidence to command your life. When you're standing in your truth and expressing it, there's no way to "play small" or dim your light.

Becky Norwood's book demonstrates she is one of the most powerful women standing strong in her conviction to change the world for survivors and inspire hope. *We Choose to Thrive* offers excellent resources to help any person navigate the feeling of being alone, ashamed, and a victim. I feel a deep connection to Becky, not only because of our shared background of abuse, but because we are both committed to support the transformation of survivors to thrivers.

In this enlightening book, you will discover how any seemingly insurmountable circumstance can be transformed through the power of your voice. Each "thriver" has exposed her deepest heartache, greatest struggles, and highest achievements to support you in your healing and growth. The variety of ways each person has gone from surviving to thriving is inspiring and uplifting, not to mention so real that you can't help but decide to follow their lead and THRIVE!

Chapter 1

Introduction

by Becky Norwood

"It takes far more courage to walk away from a bad situation than to stay in it. To stay is familiar. To leave is to walk into uncharted and unknown waters, and indeed that can be frightening."

~Becky Norwood

In these pages, you will find stories of women who, just like you or someone you know, has encountered, oftentimes at a very early age abuse that no one should ever have to experience.

I have my own story, one that took me until age 60 to finally gain the courage to speak up about. I published my story in August of 2016, "The Woman I Love: Surviving, Healing and Thriving after a Childhood of Sexual, Emotional and Physical Abuse."

Since then, I have met way too many women and men both who have experienced incredible abuses in their lives. Some have had the courage to speak up; some are just now arriving at that place where they want to take the action necessary to heal.

Sadly, our world does have a problem, a huge one at that. Statistics are all over the place and far from accurate, but it is estimated 1 out of 3 girls and 1 out of 5 boys are affected by this dreadful epidemic.

I wonder, truly wonder how many have gone to their grave with the deep, dark secret still haunting them. Why? For most it is because of the shame, the fear and the sadness of being so alone in their pain.

If you are starting down the path to healing, no matter what stage, our united message is that you are not alone.

We do not choose to live with a victim mentality. We choose to thrive, and as such, we are joining arms to spread the message that you too can heal and thrive.

Will you join us as a force of change we need in our world?

Only by healing, growing strong, and uniting can we create the awareness of this terrible epidemic that is plaguing our world.

We heal in many different ways. There is no one right way to heal, but the right thing to do is to heal. Heal for yourself, for your families, and for our world. Will you join us in this We Choose to Thrive revolution?

In the pages that follow, you will read the brief stories of women from all walks of life and from several different countries. This particular book centers on the stories of women. We acknowledge that men have their stories as well, stories that they need to give voice to and we honor them for that. When the time is right, we will be releasing another book, this one with stories from our male counterparts.

While the topic for many in this book has been childhood sexual abuse, it also includes domestic violence during adulthood. We want to be clear that no matter what kind of abuse, or when it happened, abuse is abuse. There is no measuring device that can measure the impact and intensity of abuse, nor how that abuse is processed individually.

Because we are all so unique, some may appear to have weathered better than another. Many went through hell and back to finally make the conscious decision to rise above their past. The bottom line is that we have chosen to heal, be well and thrive.

What is also true for many survivors is that our patterns of healing often come after a long struggle with some sort of addiction. Those addictions vary from sexually inappropriate behaviors, drug and alcohol addictions, suicidal tendencies, cutting (self mutilation) to depression. I call it sadness addiction…the inability to simply be happy in life.

There came a time when we've simply grown weary of the nonsense, the pain, and decided to make a change.

Know that change often does not come overnight, nor does it have a once changed always changed magic pill. It is something that takes determination, desire and diligence, as there will always be triggers that can hit at unexpected moments.

Many of us have said we have a PhD from the school of hard knocks and experience. As we have healed, we change that to PhD from the school of the MOST fortunate. We are alive and here today to tell our stories.

Senseless abuse at the hands of someone we should have been able to trust, or senseless abuse at the hands of a stranger, leaves its scars. But we do not have to stay there.

We CAN be the force for change in our world!

Are you ready? Are you willing to join arms to stand up, speak out to break down the walls of silence and let go of the secrets of your past? Are you ready to rise up and become a force for change…change that is so desperately needed in our world?

Reach out to us at www.TheWomanILove.com, and join us on our Facebook page: https://www.facebook.com/thewomanilove1/

You will notice as you read this book that we do not go into the sordid details on the abuse we suffered. We mention it and move on. We move on to talk about what we did to begin our healing process. We talk about the tools and resources we tapped into. We talk about our mindset. We talk about what we would say to someone just beginning to wake up to answer the call to live life fully.

Why is that? Because we have found that dwelling on the pain of the past does nothing for us. You've heard the saying: "What we focus on expands." Well if we focus on, dwelling day in and day out on the horrible things we have experienced, if we live in regret, sadness, hatred, fear, and looking back, we simply cannot move forward. It is superbly difficult to rise above it and feel joy.

Deliberately, catch your thoughts and do something, say something that will change your focus. Direct your energy to feeling good, give it your focus and good will come.

We strive to put our attention on the beautiful lives we are now creating for ourselves. We have learned self love. We have learned to honor ourselves.

Think about how you feel when you are feeling down. It's certainly is not fun! Then think about how you feel and respond when you are having a great day. It is remarkably different.

We know that we have had to become selfish in a good way. We know that in order for us to heal we need to focus on what we want, not what we don't want. We are progressing in our lives with the goal of being more. More tuned in, tapped in, and turned on to who we truly are inside of us. The part of you that is love, joyful, happy…tune into that!

Experience the leverage, the advantage, the power that comes from utilizing the energy that creates worlds. As you begin to care more about how you feel, first and foremost, you will begin to follow your joy, and then your impulses and intuition to the actions you will take, and this will bring you healing.

Focus on you. Cater to the emotions in you that feel good. Create for yourself your power thoughts and mantras that you utilize daily.

Know that in being selfishly in love with ourselves, we have more to give to our families, our communities and our world. If we are not well inside, mentally, emotionally, and spiritually, we have nothing to give.

Also, check out the incredible resources in your own communities and online. We have listed the resources throughout the chapters of this book and again at the end of the book for easy of reference.

And notably…If you are actively facing abuse in this moment, Do NOT DELAY! Seek out help in your local community immediately.

Here's to your wellness, healing, and thriving!

My own Personal Story: **http://amzn.to/2i0pn5h**

"The irony is that we attempt to disown our difficult stories to appear more whole or more acceptable. But our wholeness, even our wholeheartedness actually depends on the integration of all of our experiences, including the falls.

~Brené Brown

"Don't let the darkness from your past block the light of joy in your present. What happened is done. Stop giving time to things which no longer exist, when there is so much joy to be found here and now."

~Karen Salmasohn

Chapter 2

Jo Dibblee

"My mission in life is not merely to survive, but to thrive; and to do so with some passion, some compassion, some humor, and some style."

~ Maya Angelou

Jo Dibblee resides in Sooke, British Columbia, is an astute business woman and is passionate about helping women find success in life, love, and business. Her company Frock-Off serves women business owners. She shares her story to create change and you will understand why. Her mantra is that we must stand ON our story, not IN our story.

Jo's Story:

I was born into a family of severe mental trauma, and over time the foster system got involved. I became a witness for the RCMP (police) in a highly publicized criminal investigation. It was a cold case which lasted for 35+ years. At fifteen I was sexually assaulted by a foster parent who went on to murder a little girl I knew. I was in hiding for 35 years.

I know what you are doing now, and the impact you have on women's lives. What prompted the change for you?

When I went through my second divorce, it was yet another trauma in what seemed endless. Divorce is the death of not only a marriage but of the future. It was yet another blow while I continued to live in hiding from a man who became a serial killer.

The very fabric of who I was…was always in question. I lived a lie after lie to stay alive. During my time in hiding I had had 19 names, and I had moved dozens of times. My then husband had no real idea of who I was. The long and the short of it was that the second divorce was the demarcation time in my life. When the RCMP had shown up asking for someone else ... that someone else had been me and that began the unraveling of my many stories. In 2005 things were bleak and by midyear, it was all over. Less than two years later all that was left was the waiting period for yet another divorce, and I was broken and exhausted - tired of all the loss and sick of living a life of fear, shame, and guilt.

It was Feb. 28, 2007, my girlfriend and I were out taking a walk; I was still in hiding, and she asked me what I would do differently if my life could look different. I said I would "Frock-Off." While she thought we were talking about divorce, and we were, I was also talking about my entire life!

Interestingly, that later became the title of my memoir. A book that I would take five years to write and publish!

That was my demarcation day. Enough was enough. I had spent so many years of my life in hiding - not being who I truly was and the price had been high. And now, I was getting divorced again. It was a devastating time, but it was also a time of reckoning and reclamation for me. I had crossed that line, and I was done living that way.

Where are you now in your healing journey?

Now! What a difference! I am finally free! And I have relocated back to the province I fled 35 years ago. For years I yearned to return.

I wrote my book Frock Off: Living Undisguised in 2013 and I went from being visibly invisible, meaning (in plain sight but living under many different aliases) to highly visible and successful.

It was because I said enough was enough - I stood and took back my life and found the courage to write my book- to tell my story. It was because I stood up. It was because I wrote my book. It was because of the courage and conviction I found to tell my story.

The truth is that if we want to live fully, we have no choice we must claim our life. The reason I am where I am now is that I said YES and in the absence of proof!

What did you tap into as a resource or tool that helped you make that change?

In my mid-thirties, I had tried to speak with counselors, sharing bits and pieces of my childhood - the parts that safe to share. Often the counselors would break down and be upset for me, and I would end up comforting them. In retrospect, it is interesting that that did help me because I came to understand that it was ok for me to be sad and lost at times. Seeing them sad, showed me that it was not normal to live that way.

Ultimately my solace came the through my writing of the book. It was a healing journey. So, to answer your question, for me, it was the writing of my book. I wrote it long hand, and it took me five years to write it. At the time I was not sure I would publish - remaining terrified that my perpetrator would find me and "finish the job," as he had said those many years ago.

Fear is powerful so much so that when I wrote, I hid chapters of my book under the drawer liners of my dresser. Not only was there the fear of him finding me, but what about someone else reading it? What would they think, how could they understand?

All of us will find solace and healing in different ways. The bottom line is that we are here to make an impact in the world and we cannot truly do that until we heal.

Word by word and chapter by chapter the healing continued. And the once overwhelming and all powerful story started to become just that a story. It was going from being my secret, shameful story to something that was real and albeit sad no longer held the same power. When I decided to publish the book, it became another facet of my healing.

Releasing that story by letting someone else read it was incredible. The day came to send it for editing and when I did it was both freeing and terrifying. The feedback was immediate - a woman who I trusted was so moved so impacted by the story she vowed to help me and committed to working side by side with me. She was determined to help me get it out to the world. Her genuine dedication and commitment changed my fear to conviction.

Since leaving Corporate Canada and opening my own business in 2001, I have worked with women in business - elevating, engaging and helping them move from secret to success. What was interesting, to me, is that the same women I thought had it all suffered from self-doubt, shame, fear, and self-judgment too. Seeing this created a new perspective - It became real for me.

What would you say to someone starting this journey of healing?

What I know for sure is that you must: Stand ON your story and not IN it. We are here…we have crossed over the fear and guilt, which is its' own rebirth. If you are struggling, know that you are not here for that story. It's a part of who you are the stories make you who you are. Our stores create connection they make us empathetic, approachable, relatable and caring.

However, this does not mean it is our lot in life we were not born to live that story. It is merely one chapter of our lives. That was just what happened at the time. Although not all of us are called to tell our story as we are in this book - that is a personal decision only you can make.

What is relevant is what we do with it. I believe that we are here to serve and do something so much bigger than what happened.

Sadly many take their dreams (because of their stories) to the grave, do not let that be you. You are NOT your story. You need to stand on it, not in it and that is how we thrive.

Do what you were intended to do. You know it. It's is in your heart.

Those that make the decision to stand up and move forward move obstacles, and doors open. That changes everything.

One person can change the legacy in a family. You can choose to do the work, and heal - be the example and touch other lives. Simply being free and happy changes the vibration of life and there is glory in the story. Heal and be well, and it will impact the world.

Ultimately my story was a story of parents who were ill and a foster parent gone terribly wrong. No child should be afraid to go home or be exploited at the hand of another. Home is supposed to be safe.

When we can stand and take back our lives, and we choose to do so, we encourage others to do the same. I am committed to being change, by helping 13.1 million women - it's real and what is happening here is powerful.

Is it your time to stand up, step up and be the change in your life? Deciding to stand creates ripples of change impacting not only you but those you know - your family, your community, and society.

My story is not a comparison and measuring of better or worse. That's not relevant what is relevant is you and your life matters!

Do whatever it takes to live the life you dream. Reexamine where you are right now and determine where you want to be. If we remain stuck in our stories, we do not bring joy to our lives. Come to the table ready to take what you need to create the life that you desire and yearn. Identify and move past what is going on in your life.

Create a new story for yourself!

It begins with us and our relationship with self. We can't get right with ourselves if we carry around the past.

So let it go.

Listen to Jo Dibblee's Video Interview:
https://youtu.be/GQWpr9vEp38

Jo Dibblee's books:

Frock-Off: Living Undisguised, A Memoir
http://amzn.to/2ixiVQs

Best Kept Secrets to Success in Love, Life and Business
http://amzn.to/2ixedlP

Jo's website: **http://www.frock-off.com**

12 for 12 Speakers Program:
http://www.frock-off.com/12for12-membership/

Chapter 3

Cheryl-Ann Webster

"I am in the world to change the world."

~ Kathe Kollwitz (1867-1945)

C heryl-Ann hails from beautiful Victoria, British Colombia. Better known as the "Boob Lady" by the younger generation, she is well known for the Beautiful Woman Project, being an artist first and a speaker and facilitator second. Cheryl-Ann uses her art as the backdrop on stage, on a screen or in an exhibit as she encourages her viewers to start to explore who they are and what is shaping their life.

You will enjoy our interview with her.

I am thriving because art saved my life! Today, I use self expression and my process of ART: Awareness-Resilience-Transformation, to help individuals and groups to thrive.

My message has always been about using art to encourage others to be able to explore some of the things that impact them, and on occasion

21

hold themselves back. Even more importantly, to celebrate what makes them who they are.

It is my belief that we must share our stories, not just to help other people heal, but that first and foremost, so that we can get our story out of our physical body. So that we can see our story external from ourselves, and to be able to understand better how that story is shaping us.

I've chosen to share my stories publicly so the lessons I have learned maybe useful in the healing journey of others. I started down this path because as a little girl, I was silenced. I lived in a home that was not safe and experienced many forms of abuse and, as with many children, I assumed what I was experiencing was normal. I was a vocal child and tried to speak to other people about what was happening to me as if that was normal. Obviously, I was silenced quickly, told "little girls should be seen and not heard". The problem was I had a lot to say and many emotions to express.

As I was not a naughty child, I did not lash out in a way that would get attention. Instead, I quietly started to doodle with pen and paper. Without many art supplies to tap into at home, I drew on scraps of paper to express my feelings. However, school was a mecca for stationery, so rather than writing essays, the lined paper became my canvas.

That was the beginning of it all for me. I soon discovered that people did not necessarily know what I was trying to say, so I got 'told off' frequently for doodling on everything, but it made me feel better. And even though I may have scribbled all day and others did not know what I was saying, I was expressing myself and art had become my voice for my inner thoughts, feelings AND fears. I certainly was not a good artist; in fact, I failed art in high school because I wasn't following the curriculum. When they wanted me to paint a bouquet of flowers, I was scribbling scenes that were expressing pain and hurt. Unfortunately, my art was not understood.

Today, perhaps it would be different. Maybe someone would have understood, spoken to me, asked the right questions and helped me. But the awareness was simply not there in the 1980s. What remains interesting to me is that my abuse did not cause external bruising. But apparently, I was often bruised as a child and school officials called me into the office, and asked if anyone had hit me. I quite honestly said, "NO, I'm a princess and I bruise so easily".

Now I wonder why they only asked about bruising and hitting - that told me hitting was wrong and so people should not hit you. But if anyone had actually asked me if someone was touching me, or if I was being treated poorly at home, maybe I would have told them everything. My story may have been very different. Back in England, at that time, talking of anything other than physical abuse was extremely taboo. You did not speak about it with anyone. Not your friends, not your family NOBODY!

So I stayed silent, burying my story deep within me, until I came to Canada (in 1996). It was only then, when I was in a wonderful, stable, loving relationship that, my story refused to stay inside. So instead of feeling that life was great, I crashed like a lead balloon. It was very confusing to feel safe and comfortable, and happy and yet break down... feeling like my world was crumbling.

Now I know, my story surfaced because I DID feel safe. So safe, my story had a space to be revealed. I returned to creating art; in fact, I accelerated my creative expression and gave my story a voice.

My husband and I built a studio, and while our friends and family expected me to make beautiful art pieces - vases and such, I created sculptures of women with titles such as "trapped" and "healing." With each piece I created I reclaimed my life. Since then, my art has become my visual voice to speak for me and for all who have been silenced.

In your healing journey, what would you say has worked best for you?

Without a doubt, art and my process of ART - deepening self Awareness, strengthening my Resilience and taking Transformational steps towards thriving in life have not only helped, but truly saved me.

For me sharing my story so publicly has been empowering and there are many ways in which others can 'share' their story. However, openly sharing is only one option and not the best option for everyone. There are times when it is not safe to share with the world, nor the proper thing to do for many reasons.

However, keeping a story buried inside can cause a great deal of emotional and even physical damage. It took me a while to figure out how best to share my story. When I first started sharing, I just 'spit' it at people, then, I would leave them not knowing what to do with my story. I felt better, but was it fair for them?

Implementing the ART to Life:

I suggest that at any and all points of your healing journey, always explore inward, gaining more awareness of what the effects are of what has happened to you. Discover what is still sitting within you that is still silent. Ask many questions. How have the parts of your story impacted or shaped you? Did it make you stronger and more vocal? Is it holding you back from feeling happy or enjoying a great and passionate relationship, for instance? Are there voids in your memory, or in sensing your body? Is there something that just does not feel right in your life?

Take that awareness and look at it all in a safe and secure way. There are many ways that you can do that. Find out what works for you. Try writing a journal, speaking to a therapist, taking a dance class, or go on a retreat. Start small. Take a piece of your story out from deep inside you. Explore it. Break it down. Take it apart, come to understand your own comfort with it, then either put it back if you are not ready to face it, or dialogue with it - paint it, write it, scream it, and in your own way, release it. The story will not be gone but its strength will wane.

Of course, because of my own background, I recommend doing this through art - through visual expression. Remember, it doesn't mean you need to be gifted in art at all! Why art?

Because, there are so many emotions and experiences, that we do not have words for. And for so many of us, our story started when we were young and our experiences and feelings were more complex than our vocabulary. Even now, I believe a vocabulary does not exist that can adequately give voice to our heart and soul. While in art and creativity we have an unlimited number of colors, textures, shapes and materials that can speak for us. Whether it is gathering together scrap paper, putting paint on a canvas, taking a bottle and safely breaking it and putting the shards back together with glue, there are endless ways we can express ourselves, our stories and feelings.

It is in the act of going beyond words that we find there is a "vocabulary" for every emotion and experience we have felt, continue to feel and continue to experience.

In addition to creative expression through art, I have found that my process of ART - Awareness, Resilience and Transformation has benefitted all my clients. For example, a client who is very outgoing and who has acted out as a coping mechanism, became aware that a silent retreat would lead her to explore inward and discover that the resilience she has in other areas of life could be used to feel safe at the retreat.

Please note that, although such a retreat may be a pivotal moment, the long term transformation may be more subtle. In contrast, I am aware it was my enforced silencing that led me to become a public speaker and an advocate.

Overall, I encourage my clients to deepen their awareness of their story, to strengthen their resilience to its impact and take the transformational steps that feel right for them. Together we explore, express and evolve through my one-on-one coaching, or group facilitation.

My website is **http://www.cherylannwebster.com/**

Cheryl-Ann Webster's Video Interview:
https://youtu.be/2GQ2lFMhnyo

Website: **http://www.CherylAnnWebster.com**

Cheryl-Ann's Beautiful Woman Project:
https://www.facebook.com/beautifulwomenproject

Chapter 4

Traci Bogan

I wish you a happy life! It's your time to Dream it. Plan it. Live it! Enjoy the Adventure!

~Traci Bogan

After only 11 minutes of the QuantumPathic® Energy Method (QPEM), I had the single most profound release and breakthrough I've ever experienced around the issues of being sexually abused as a child. Those 11 minutes were worth more than all the tens of thousands of dollars I'd spent for a decade on therapy and every kind of anti-depressant, A-Z. This was at a free introductory lecture! I'd heard about it only 24 hours earlier from someone I'd just met and I felt drawn to go.

I walked in and sat in the front row. Without even a hello, Sherry Anshara walked up to me and said, "You have Hashimoto's disease." True. I did have the autoimmune disorder. But how did she know at first glance, I wondered? "I can see it in your neck," she said. "Would you like to know why you created that for yourself?"

Seriously?? I thought to myself. I was puzzled! She said I was sexually abused as a child and didn't have a voice to speak my truth, thereby creating Hashimoto's disease, TMJ, and chronic back pain. She stated, "Every ache and pain is your body attempting to talk to you. Pay attention. Every piece of illness is your body attempting to talk to you. Most of the time, we just don't listen. We cover up the pain with Band-Aids and medicate ourselves to death. Now, are you ready to release this, Traci?"

Yes, I was ready! She was right. I was sexually abused as a child from age 5 until 14. I had what seemed like a lifetime of keeping that silence inside me. It was my dirty little secret. I always felt inadequate and used to pray at bedtime every night for God to make me "normal".

Then somewhere around the age of 20, I told my best friend, Amy. She said I shouldn't have to bear the weight of this on my shoulders any more. I didn't do anything wrong. One day, I picked up the phone and called one of the two uncles who were my perpetrators and said, "I remember what you did to me. I want you to acknowledge it and I want an apology." I can still hear his words and remember the shakiness in his voice as he uttered, "Yah, I'm sorry for that. You guys are the only family I got. You're not gonna tell anyone now are ya? Are we good now?" Yeah, I was good with that for a while. He apologized and acknowledged it. I didn't need to tell my family. That apology was all that I required.

But Amy further encouraged me to tell my family and not hang onto their secret any longer. I just couldn't. I was so ashamed. I felt old enough to know better and quite frankly, the attention of the abuse felt good. So I asked her to tell my parents. They were shocked. After they confronted my uncles, one of them said, "I would cut off my right arm if I could take it back. I'm so deeply sorry." The other uncle, who initially apologized to me on the phone, denied it publicly until his untimely death by suicide last April. It divided and divorced our family. But I know and he knew. Today, it no longer matters to me who believes it. It happened.

I spent the entire decade of the 90's so lost and disconnected from my body, my past, and my purpose. I was completely directionless. I self-sabotaged everything I did and could not maintain any kind of long-term relationship. I pickled my liver in alcohol, and lived just to have fun. I jumped from therapist to therapist, from counselors to preachers, from psychologists to psychiatrists, from EMDR therapy to personal development seminars and ropes courses. I was desperately looking for someone or something to "fix" me and make me feel better and whole and relevant.

Anti-depressants made me homicidal and suicidal. "I want to jump off my balcony right now. I want to shoot the people who did this to me and f***ed up my life," I said to the therapist while living in Hawaii. "You have to help me. Stop me. Do something. Get me off of these pills before I do something stupid. This drug is effecting my brain and making me think things I normally don't think. I'm just not me. I will not take these pills another moment longer."

That was the last time I ever took an anti-depressant or saw a therapist. I was always looking for something outside of me.

In addition, I spent two years lobbying, and finally succeeded in a crusade to increase the criminal statute of limitations for sex crimes on children in the State of Wisconsin. My grassroots effort was dubbed 'The Bogan bill'. Though its sister bill is the one that was actually enacted into law, it was still gratifying to be a part of a state-wide movement, that was bigger than me and will outlive me.

I thought that working to pass the Bogan Bill was my cleansing, my clearing, and my healing. "Okay, we're done with this now. This is never going to affect me again." It simply wasn't true. I went more than two decades of my life with 'Victim' branded on my forehead. It wasn't until I embarked on reading and researching things that felt correct for me, that led me to self-healing, which ultimately led me to Sherry Anshara and the QuantumPathic® Center of Consciousness. Here I was introduced to the QuantumPathic® Energy Method (QPEM).

Out of all my therapists from Wisconsin to Hawaii, no one ever suggested the answers were within. Imagine the time, effort, money, and experience I could have saved had somebody shown me how to connect with my body and assisted me in recognizing and awakening my own inner power.

This is what carried me through: I submersed myself in personal development books and tapes and meditations. I would fall asleep listening to subliminal and motivational messages and re-loop them all night long for eight hours straight. I would listen to them while cleaning the house, showering, getting ready for work, and driving in the car. I became obsessed with inputting good and positive things into my brain, soul, and being. This led me to yoga. That led me to eating cleaner, or a little more whole.

This then led me to working out, taking care of my body, and exercising my heart. Then I was led to read deeper books and attend personal development seminars to learn about expanding my consciousness. This ultimately led me to the QuantumPathic® Energy Method (QPEM) out here in Arizona.

How did I get to Arizona? Two years ago I was sitting in my office in Wisconsin. It was a chilly October morning. I had my feet on my desk and was looking at my "Dreams Can". It's a product I created. I sell them at my motivational speaking events, workshops, and seminars. Inside of this Dreams Can I have about 700 cards on which I hand-wrote everything I desire to be, do, share, and experience in my lifetime.

Every couple of months when I feel so inclined, I reach in the Can and randomly draw something out. That day I pulled the card that said, "Go winter somewhere warm for 90 days." On the back were five choices from Arizona to Florida to Costa Rica. I closed my eyes and said, "Eeny meeny miny mo," and my finger landed on Arizona.

Fourteen days later, I got on an airplane with no business contacts, connections, or resources, hardly knowing anyone. It was a fun self-imposed challenge to see what I would and could create for my life and business.

My dream was to winter some place warm and run my speaking and coaching business from anywhere in the world with just a laptop and a cell phone. This was my sure-fire test to prove that my coaching program worked because I was living the adventure and achieving the results live in front of my social media audience. I came here with that one desire but ended up with a whole new discovery and awareness.

I now feel that my energy drew me to Arizona just to experience the QuantumPathic® Energy Method (QPEM). In such a short time, I released something I didn't consciously know was still frustrating me and holding me back from playing bigger. After all, another decade had passed and by all accounts, I was living my dream life. I had backpacked around the world, written a few books, had a winter and summer condo, vacationed 100 days a year, and was running a successful speaking and coaching business for entrepreneurs.

I had come a long way from the factory job I started off with during my turmoil and I was proud of all my achievements. The only thing missing was a loving and committed relationship, the lack of which I blamed on my busy life-on-the-move lifestyle. I was "good" and things were "good."

And then I found the QuantumPathic® Energy Method (QPEM) or it found me! I discovered a whole new set of tools, a whole new practical application for connecting with my body, and a whole new method of releasing and cleansing that I didn't even know I required, and I got clear on why my relationships weren't working and what was holding me back from really achieving my own boldest goals and most daring dreams. I didn't know what I didn't know. And then I did.

If I could press a button or take a pill and make my sexual abuse go away, as if it never happened, or make my sexuality, which I've denied my entire life, disappear, I wouldn't do it. It is a piece of who I am and I embrace the whole, bona fide me. My intention is to pass on the lessons and knowledge as best as I can through my own experiences. And share with you from which you can grow and be prosperous, to be inspired and empowered. Whatever your demons are or whatever skeletons you are hiding in your closet, you too can move past and grow beyond them. Today is the perfect day for you to make a new choice and choose a new life or a new way.

I feel like my soul has emerged for the very first time. My soul has taken its very first breath of life with a new heartbeat into my life. After all the years I spent soul searching to find some method to bring ease, peace, and balance into my life, it was finally met when I discovered the

QuantumPathic® Energy Method (QPEM), which led me to ME. I met ME, my true self and my Perfect Child Within, (PCW) and they melded into one. It all arrived in perfect time.

Now that I am here, it is a beautiful feeling. I feel an inner peace and unity that I have never felt before. I am whole and perfectly expanding. I am connected with my body and my life purpose, which is leading entrepreneurs to achieve their boldest goals, most daring dreams, and live their authentic, empowered life through my professional speaking and coaching services.

Here is how I start my day:

Every morning when I wake up, I do the QuantumPathic® Energy Method (QPEM) process of connecting with my body, which I learned in the Healing at Your Core workshop. As a result, my day flows and my attitude escalates. Everything improves. My relationships with clients, family, and friends are better because I'm operating from a different frequency and vibration. I start my day and my business calls from a place of heartness and intention. I am the one who creates my day, my schedule, and my life. Life no longer runs and controls me.

First, I open up my crown chakra and lay down. I feel the energy flow to my fingers and toes. Then I connect, acknowledge, and thank my body and ask what my body requires for the day. The body knows all the answers.

If I am experiencing pain, I ask my body:
What does the space or place in the pain look like?
How old am I in the space, place, or pain?
What is the root cause of the pain?
What message is the pain sharing with me?

Then I am being the process to honor, release, and clear the pain. I always choose to experience a release and deep connection with my body and myself. Because I connect to my body and acknowledge my body, my consciousness is coming from my heartness instead of my thinky, thinky brain.

Here is one of the particular breakthroughs I had while implementing the QuantumPathic® Energy Method (QPEM) at home. I have had left hip, SI Joint, and low back pain for twenty plus years. So one morning, I chose to get to the root cause to clear this pain and discomfort. I began with my throbbing hip, cradling it with my hands and asked my body the questions I learned in the Healing at Your Core workshop.

This particular day, through my mind's eye, I noticed my five-year-old self was in a cage, like the ones they use for dogs. The cage was lying next to the right side of my body, which is the male manifesting side of the body.

Every morning for weeks, in my mind's eye, I'd walk over and coerce or drag my five-year-old self out of this cage and stand her up. Because she's been in this cage, she is like a puppet with wobbly legs. I shake her until her legs get strong enough to stand on her own. Then she stands firmly and cheerfully walks to the left side of my body. And we start our day.

I was getting so frustrated seeing my five-year-old self inside of this cage. Then one morning, I started swearing and said to the five-year-old *ME* in the cage, "I do not require you to be in this cage anymore! You get your ass out of this cage yourself. You are strong enough to get out of the cage yourself! DO IT NOW! Get your ass out here now!" Every day, my five-year-old self would get out of the cage. I'd send her to the left side, which is the female creator side of the body. Then we'd start our day.

Then I attended my second workshop, Head to the Heart. This is where I had some of the most profound breakthroughs of my entire life. The Monday after the workshop, I sat down to do my morning meditation and there was no cage!

The five-year-old child who I had connected with during the weekend workshop experience was in the shape of a starburst with her fists raised above her head in "victory" and her legs stretched out below her. She was ever so perfectly positioned in my solar plexus/heart area. Like a perfect-fitting puzzle piece facing the world with me, centered in my chest. She had a huge smile on her face. I was beaming too!

That was my Perfect Child Within, (PCW). We were truly connected in this moment. It was a new feeling inside, a new layer of strength and it was bold and beautiful. I had the greatest sense of purposefulness and love for her. This was the biggest shift I had so far in working with the QuantumPathic® Energy Method (QPEM), applying the tools I learned. A sense of purpose, a feeling of connection, and an expansion of consciousness happened.

About a week later, my five-year-old self kept showing up, just as she had in my daily meditations. I was always so happy to see her. She was still cage-less, but she was lessening and fading. Sometimes she was happy, sometimes she was sad. And then, she was just sad.

I didn't feel her power or *the* power anymore. Here was this little girl dragging her feet and bowing her head before me in our morning meditations. I was frustrated again. When I asked her what was bothering her, it always came back to her pain of being sexually abused and not being believed by some family members. Why did the same sexual abuse story keep coming up in every area of my body we chose to work on during the body scan? Why!!

"I'm sick and tired of this story," I said to Sherry Anshara during a phone call. "I don't require it anymore. I'm releasing it. I don't want to talk about it anymore and how it has affected me. I am done with it! How much frigging longer can this take? Will this abuse continue to affect, effect, and infect my life and continue to rob me of fully living?!"

Then Sherry Anshara said, "Instead of demeaning this five-year-old Traci for showing up again because she is in pain, crouch down on your knees, get face to face with her and ask her what message she has for you."

When I asked my five-year-old Perfect Child Within she said, "I require you to believe in me, to love me, to trust me, and to get out of our way. I have known what to do from the beginning. I have gotten us this far, NOT you!" She pointed a finger firmly at me, the adult. "Your adult Childish Adult Ego is standing in the way of your relationships, businesses, finances, wellness…everything, because you make a decision, then you second guess yourself and try to change courses. You are not making choices. You are making emotional decisions."

"Me, your Perfect Child Within, says to you…You don't trust in yourself or *me*. You don't believe in yourself or *me*. You are the one who does not feel worthy…and that is your issue, not mine! I know what to do. I know we are worthy. If you would get out of your own way, surrender and trust, I, your Perfect Child Within can take charge of our life from here. We meld as *all*, not *one*. We are *Allness*."

My five-year-old Perfect Child Within put me in my place. She called me on my stuff. I embraced her. It was a beautiful moment. I honored and thanked her for standing up for our truth, for not allowing me to get in the way any longer. For reminding me if I trust and surrender to the highest and greatest good of our consciousness, all will be provided and all will be perfect and all will show up in divine order.

This is what led to my five-year-old Perfect Child Within, in my solar plexus/heart area, smiling and beaming because we are now whole, we are now *Allness*. We are connected. Before, I felt her as a separate person from me. Now I know we are together and we are *Allness*. She is me. We are this strength and this divine source energy.

In the past, when I went through the QuantumPathic® Energy Method (QPEM) connecting process, the opening of the solar plexus/heart, I always experienced two sources conflicting with each other. One was anger; the other was Source energy.

I realized I liked hanging onto the anger because anger was my greatest motivator. I could be prodded and pushed to anger. Some days it's like boiling water. It only takes one degree to move from hot water to boiling water. When it reaches that one degree to boiling anger this is when I propel into action. I call it my boiling anger ball. I make things happen when we get to this temperature.

That's the space from which I created the 'Bogan Bill'. From this anger space, I backpacked around the world. Then I wrote my first book because nobody believed I could. Then I went to college at age 35 and got straight A's. Then I moved to Hawaii with $800 in my pocket with the same anger. Through this anger, I was motivated by that one degree to the boiling anger point. I realized I liked it. I wanted to hang onto it.

That last weekend at the Head to the Heart workshop, I cleared the anger to only allow that Source energy. There was nothing in my solar plexus/heart but this ball, a deep blue color that doesn't exist on Earth. It is a color that had sound, a color that had a heartbeat, a color that was alive or was life. This giant globe was churning in a slow roaring motion. It looked like the shape and size of Earth with a more piercing presence.

As it swung in a slow rotation, my five-year-old self was facing me, then my adult self, then my child self, then my adult self, slowly spinning round and round in deafening slow motion. I could hear the heartbeats of my five-year-old child and my adult self merge.

I felt alive for the very first time in my life. The giant globe went from the blue-looking Earth to this massive energy ball that was the color of Saturn. Her power and brilliance intensified before my being until I felt her in my core, and then as my core. We were Allness! Source energy! Pure love!

In this moment, I realized that my whole life I had been attempting to control the movement of this force, through my boiling anger ball, instead of surrendering to or allowing the power, this beautiful Source energy to move me. I realized with Real Eyes that I had been attempting to control and manipulate this energy instead of allowing it to move me into flow.

My Power, my Source energy vs. the force of my Childish Adult Ego is my boiling anger ball and the pain of conflict within me. This conflict and pain led me to purpose. I went from breathing to being breath. I achieved going from life's motions to living my life fully. From being angry to being love. From being a victim to being a thriver!

I've had such incredible transformation and expansion in my life since implementing the QuantumPathic® tools and the practical applications of the tools that I learned through the QuantumPathic® Energy Method (QPEM). As a result, I have referred more than 100 family, friends, and clients to the workshops and one-on-one sessions with Sherry Anshara in just nine months.

Several of my friends have gotten on airplanes from all corners of the country to experience the workshop, sight unseen, with few questions asked, just based on my 'word' that this was genuine, real, and worth it.

A Gift for You!

10 Day Transformational Dare: I am gifting you 10 days of transformational activities and worksheets that will assist you to creating your authentic empowered life! Simply text **dare** to 96000 to begin your Transformation NOW! **www.TraciBogan.com**

QuantumPathic® Energy Method by Sherry Anshara:
http://quantumpathicinstitute.com/

Traci's Video Interview: **https://youtu.be/I0d6hwphuLk**

Chapter 5

Karin Tyson

"One thing that was told to me when I began this journey was that being a survivor was sort of like a club. Becoming a member was a horrible ordeal, but you will never find a group of more understanding and loving people who don't judge and will help you heal in whatever way they can."

~Karin Tyson

It's amazing how many people there are have been through this. I know that is everywhere, but it never ceases to amaze me how many survivors I meet.

I was born and raised in Columbus, Georgia and have lived in Smith Station Alabama pretty much all my life.

Recently, I graduated with my bachelor's at Auburn University in 2015 with a focus in political science, international relations; specifically, in the Middle East and North Africa. At first I wanted to pursue my masters in Egypt, at the American University in Cairo, but with a husband and child at home, I decided to stay local and get my MPA degree at Auburn.

I am finishing up my last year now focusing in non-profit management: sexual violence prevention and women's reproductive health.

Securing my internship at the Sexual Assault Support Center, Inc. in Columbus, Georgia has been phenomenal. I've learned a lot about the system outside of being a survivor.

I've been really hands on especially with grant writing. I recently wrote a grant, two weeks ago, for my future position. They wanted to hire me is the median outreach coordinator and victim advocate. (At this writing Karin did get the grant and was hired!)

I am proud of myself how many issues I've been able to overcome. I had spent so much time upset and miserable with life, with anxiety being a huge issue.

It was last year that I came out talking about what happened to me. I was a relatively quiet child and I never got into trouble. One night I spent the night with a friend and her mother was out of town. She invited her boyfriend and his friend over. I knew he had some sort of attraction or affection for me, but it was not reciprocated. Looking back, I think that made him hostile. Anyway, throughout the evening he kept making passes at me. My friends went off to her room, and I became increasingly uncomfortable with him.

Finally, I got up and went to the master bedroom hoping to ditch him or for him to get the hint, but he followed me in there, shutting the door behind him. I had crawled into the bed and pull the covers over me where I laid in the fetal position on my left side facing the wall with the window beside me.

He started forcing himself on me, and I actually blacked out after a certain point. When I came to, I was pretty much a mess. My girlfriend did not want to believe me since they were friends and, of course, I was not only embarrassed, I suffered a lot of trauma and self sabotaging behavior trying to deal with the pain of it all. I never blamed her since we were children, and it was not her fault for his actions towards me.

It all came to a head when I lost my grandmother and was not dealing with the loss well. Eventually, I had to seek counseling to ease the pain, and my counselor was thorough in her analysis of me. She really steered me in the right direction. In one case, I remember my counselor asked me to write down five things I love about myself, and initially I could not think of anything! That opened my eyes to what she saw.

I have since come to learn from working at the local sexual assault support center, that sexual assault is quite an epidemic even, sadly, in families. That has helped me a lot with my healing. It also helped me to understand what some things my mother had gone through. She is a survivor of domestic violence.

I came to understand that my talents are most needed right here in my own community. I work to spread awareness of the problem. What is striking is that there is a huge incline of people with disabilities that suffer from this kind of abuse as well.

The other thing I want people to know is that there IS support out there and that often it is free or little cost and that they can remain autonomous. There is NOTHING to be ashamed about. Get the support you need.

One of the best things, yet hardest things I did for myself in the last year was a campaign I created on Facebook. I knew my family would see it. I knew my friends would see it. But I knew I needed to let others know that there is help and support. I told about what happened to me and talked about the aftermath of what happened, as well as what I've done to get better and what kind of support is available. I received many messages. Some of these were from people I did not even know, but they thanked me for having the courage to speak up.

It was like the closing of a chapter in my life and opening up this new one! It paved the way for me to get my master's degree and the work experience I now have.

Does that mean I do not have flashbacks? No. I have had some and I take medication to deal with it to this day with anxiety. I do have the amazing support of my husband, my coworkers and my bosses. I am a mother. I have learned to tap into my support systems.

I turned to an excellent resource and that is RAINN.ORG. Tap into help from the amazing resources that are out there!

Do not try to do this alone!

Karin Tyson's Video Interview:
https://youtu.be/daad9SHo1D8

RAINN chat: **https://www.rainn.org/get-help**

RAINN State laws: **https://apps.rainn.org/policy/**
(I always double check on the actual state sites to make sure there
haven't been any updates as well)

NSVRC (Love this resource site):
http://www.nsvrc.org/projects/bystander/share-your-stories

Start by believing:
http://www.startbybelieving.org/ShareYourStory.aspx

Brave Miss World:
http://www.bravemissworld.com/speak-out/share-your-story

Chapter 6

Nishea Martinez

"Stars can't shine without darkness."

~D.H. Sidebottom

You will be touched by Nishea's beautiful story of courage and determination. Her sweet spirit, along with a true grit and passion for healing is striking. Working a corporate job in program management and running her own makeup company where she takes the proceeds from the sales and teaches sexual assault and domestic violence survivors how to apply makeup and gives them products. She is also coaching strength and conditioning on top of volunteering.

When I was nine my family had to move in with my father's parents while we tried to find a new home for our expanding family (my mom was pregnant with my baby sister at the time).

My grandfather had accusations against him prior however nothing was told to my family. I was a sexually molested for years...years...the start of which was when we moved into their house at age nine, till I was about eighteen.

43

The mind is a beautiful and amazing thing, as a coping mechanism I repressed all memories of the abuse. I have dissociative disorder that still affects me to this day.

It wasn't until after the birth of my daughter where all of the memories resurfaced. All my years of depression during middle school and high school, cutting, suicidal tendencies, and bad choices of men was a direct effect from my abuse....I just never understood why, until those memories flooded back.

It was like getting hit by both a brick wall and a semi truck at the same time.

I ended up telling my parents when I was 22 and they chose to do nothing about it. They left it up to me. Some six years later, my grandfather came to my house and tried to enter. It was then that I realized that he did not understand what he had done to me.

It was at that time that I went through the process of filing a criminal complaint that went to trial. There were a number of women that came out of the woodwork at that time saying he had molested them as well. However, because of the statute of limitations, it was really just my case that could stand. The others served as character witnesses. He ended up plea bargaining and received a three year sentence but only served about a year and a half.

My goal is to bring awareness. To help people to understand that they have a choice and that they need to confront those who were supposed to be there for me and take care of me.

These issues so often get swept under the rug. My family history is so messed up. This would never have happened with my daughter.

Where are you now on your healing path?

I have released a lot of the anger around my molestation, and have forgiven. It has been years and years of therapy for me. Now it is progressing for me. My biggest issue with forgiveness is more with the members of my family that did not protect and that is a very common issue for many.

I am at peace now knowing that I did not do anything wrong. It took years to understand that nothing I could have done would have prevented him from doing what he did to me. My last step of getting out of the poor me, victim mentality was to begin helping others who are going through these same types of circumstances.

By volunteering at the YWCA and doing social assault response teams. By going through the training, it has opened my eyes to the fact that it a bigger problem than just a few select people. This is an epidemic. It is sad and disgusting. But it has become my saving grace, to learn that I am not alone. It has helped me to understand the memory repression is common.

My mom could not understand during those years why I pulled away from things that made me happy.

What has been the most positive thing you have done for yourself to overcome the trauma of your past?

It would definitely be going to court. Not necessarily the whole court process, not even testifying, but it was my impact statement. My impact statement still lifts me on the days that I feel down. On his sentencing day, I had invited people to come and hear me read it. About 25 of them showed up. Out of the 25 there were about four who stood and spoke on my behalf. Having the support was so impactful for me and helped me come out of the trauma. Even now, when I read my impact statement on my down days I have, it is the memories of that support that helps me the most.

I have learned to love myself and understand that all of my coping mechanisms are normal and I am not alone. This was by journaling, therapy, and seeking out other survivors to talk about my experiences.

What words of wisdom can you offer to those who have just begun their own journey of healing?

There are so many words. You are not alone. We tend to isolate ourselves because our internal self value has been so attacked. We try to hide ourselves away from the world, because we think no one understands.

I wish that I would have reached out or used resources more. There IS help out there. There is RAINN and the YWCA and all they do to support survivors. I wish I had used it more in my healing process. When you realize that 1 in 4 women are assaulted by the time they get out of college. But it so grossly underreported, that many of us question if those stats are closer to 1 in 2.

It's an on going process. There are great and amazing days/months and then there are horrific minutes...but surrounding yourself with people who support you and believe you helps you thru those horrific moments. Memories will flood your mind every once in awhile and reminding yourself that you survived and you are a warrior will help you get thru it.

I find that when I am stressed out it is more difficult. I find I have to be aware of myself and exercise a lot of self care so that I can maintain.

What resources can you recommend to those just beginning on their journey of healing?

"Courage to Heal Workbook" has helped me a lot and a great therapist who specializes in trauma recovery.

RAINN has incredible resources.

Journaling has been amazing for me. I've been trying to write a memoir, but so far have not been able to accomplish it. Someday I will.

Notes: Courage to Heal Workbook: For Women and Men Survivors of Child Sexual Abuse by Laura Davis **http://amzn.to/2d5vxky**

Nishea's Video Interview: **https://youtu.be/PWN_OR_Frhk**

www.sheabaebae.com

www.strengthcosmetics.com

www.instagram.com/shea.baebae.

Chapter 7

Carmel de Bertaut

"Tread Lightly"

~Carmel de Bertaut

I have had major trust issues. The abuse began when I was around seven years old. My oldest brother would come into my bedroom at night and ask to touch me. I did say no, but as a child, saying No had no impact. One day, I remember him laying me on my parent's bed, and opening my shirt. He put his hands on my chest, one hand where each breast would grow, to see if they "were growing."

Here was someone I should have been able to trust…my own brother, who is supposed to be protecting me, and instead he was hurting me. Nobody intervened in my behalf and that messed up my trust issues as well.

How did you begin down the path of healing? What did you do to start healing?

It's interesting, for a lot of years I thought it wasn't affecting me. I thought, "This happened, my gosh, terrible things happened to other people, this wasn't that bad, and it is really no big deal."

I have come to the terms with the fact that many of my emotional issues were a result of this abusive betrayal.

I didn't try to heal for a long time because I didn't think I had anything to heal from. As I got older I realized I had all these trust issues, I wasn't opening up to people, and I started believing and I started to realize this is, in part, because of what happened.

I started to read more and I just started to say out loud this happened and I need to address it and get over it and get my life back.

I finally told my family just two years ago.

I was very unsure about doing it, my brother has since died and I didn't know what kind of effect this was going to have on my siblings. But I did tell them and they were shocked, they were also very supportive.

Did that, then, help in your healing process?

It really did. My oldest sister, she's the oldest in the family, was so was very torn by it because she felt as though she had failed. She was everybody's big sister and she had failed to protect me.

Knowing that she felt like that, not that I wanted her to feel bad, but it restored something in me. Knowing that she didn't know, but she would've done something had she known made all the difference.

What do you feel was the most positive thing you have done that that has helped you in your healing process?

I think accepting that I did nothing wrong. For a lot of years I thought, I should've stopped him, I should've said, "No." I did say no, but it still happened. For years I was like, "It's my fault, I should've been more..."

I realized how incorrect all that was as I started to read more and more on the subject.

I think that knowing it wasn't my fault and I did nothing wrong, that allowed me to accept myself, again, as being a decent person.

As I healed, I began to believe in myself. I now have my BA and am working towards my MA.

What words of wisdom do you care to share with those that are just starting out, just coming to that awareness that

things are not working right and they need to come to grips with it so that they can move forward in their lives?

That there is a way past it, accept that it happened, accept that you had no control over it, you did nothing wrong, find the good in yourself and talk to somebody. Get the professional help you need.

Also, love yourself enough to go with the flow. If you need to step away from the recovery process and regroup…do so.

Is there a particular resource that you used that you could recommend to somebody?

I read "Courage to Heal" and that was really a huge help to me because I think hearing other peoples stories makes you really feel less isolated. That's another reason I want to be a part of this.

There are many books out there and many counselors can help. The important thing is that you listen to your gut.

The Courage to Heal: A Guide for Women Survivors of Child Sexual Abuse by Ellen Bass and Laura Davis. **http://amzn.to/2d2FwE1**

Also available: The Courage to Heal Workbook: For Women and Men Survivors of Child Sexual Abuse by Laura Davis **http://amzn.to/2d5vxky**

Carmel's Video Interview: **https://youtu.be/wkwqpTTOge4**

Chapter 8

Shanna Maria

"My mission in life is to not merely survive, but to thrive; and to do so with some passion, with compassion, some humor and some style."

~Maya Angelou

"Create the highest, grandest vision possible for your life, because you become what you believe."

~Oprah Winfrey

I was sexually abused by my grandfather. It began from the age of five till I was 17 years old. I was pregnant the last time that he ever tried to touch me and that instinct of protecting my unborn child came out and I told my grandfather; "Don't Ever try this again!" I was a few weeks shy of being 18 when I had my daughter.

For whatever reason, all the screaming in my head let loose verbally. It was what had been normal for me. My mother was a single mom and worked sometimes three jobs, and I was raised my grandparents.

Unless you have been brought up this way from an early age, it is difficult to understand when someone says this. It was my normal. When I rebelled against it, I beat myself up for a very long time because

I didn't understand that anybody else went through this kind of thing and I felt like it was my fault.

I beat myself up because why didn't I get away sooner? Why didn't I leave it before I did? How do you reckon with this as an adult, come to understand how it all happened, and why you couldn't leave? There are so many layers to an experience like this.

Where are you now in your healing Journey?

I am in a place I never thought I would actually come to. I mean, I always knew that I would be here, but I never really could believe I would actually be spending the majority of my life on this healing journey.

It's taken me a long time. It has been the last 15 years going through this journey. I knew there was this inner strength in me, I knew I could not just sit here and be a victim and let it take over my whole life.

Whatever that inner drive was, that inner fighter inside me is what saved me. I listened. I observed. I spent a lot of time alone with myself and was able to heal in a way I had hoped for but did not know I could achieve.

I feel very free now. I had to overcome losing my marriage as well. I've been retraining my brain, and all this stuff, but I am in a place now where I am ready to speak. I am ready to be an advocate. I've been sitting in the background for many years hoping and waiting for someone that I can relate to.

One person was Oprah, when she came out. Another person who had a big impact on me was Erin Merryn. Her book is called Stolen Innocence she was a guest on the Oprah show many years ago. She sparked something deep within me.

From this journey, I started with therapy. But I felt like once I needed more I needed more.

I needed a push. I needed so much more than I was receiving. On my own I ended up trying multiple things for my healing. Get yourself uncomfortable sometimes.

Take baby steps. There is no one right way.

I feel like it has taken a lifetime to heal.

Use art, poetry, writing, dance, music.

Self destructive tendencies are real, because our self worth has been eroded since childhood.

What would you tell someone who is just starting out on this healing journey?

Don't quit. The hardest part for me was starting. It may get harder before it gets easier.

When I first broke my silence it was so hard. I thought I was going to go to go to my grave with this secret.

I thought once I had broken my silence to my mother, it got harder. I had a panic attack. I had a lot of depression. I knew I could not quit… because it would take over me. Hold on. Don't quit.

I have now eliminated my depression, my anxiety. It does get better and healing IS possible.

It may seem like it takes forever. But now people come to me and ask how I have gotten as far as I have.

It is a day by day thing, but stick with it. Family members may or may not support us. Bear in mind this is your story and only you can heal from them. You can let it color your world and let it destroy it, or you can step up and make the changes and in turn be the change we need to see in the world. Family can be the most difficult. This is a complex issue. We are here to tell because we know that we are not the only ones out there.

It will take more of us to be the voice for the voiceless. No matter your age, break through the silence and speak, stand up and find your voice.

This is a global issue, and it is time to break the taboo. The epidemic needs to stop.

We are stronger together! When we hear others' stories we gain the strength to heal.

Erin Merryn's Book, "Stolen Innocence: Triumphing Over a Childhood Broken by Abuse: A Memoir **http://amzn.to/2iTQmNh**

Shanna Marie's Video Interview: **https://youtu.be/49Ac4Ar7OC0**

Chapter 9

Janet J. Bentley

"Be kind whenever possible; it is always possible."

~ Dalai Lama

I am a survivor of childhood sexual, emotional, religious and physical abuse that continued throughout my life. I was molested by my father from the age of 4. At age 9, my father watched as I was raped by his drug dealer as his payment for drugs. At age 13, I was molested and raped by a senior in high school, also an elder from the church I attended, resulting in an abortion. There were molestations by my uncle, a neighbor and other drinking friends of my parents.

My whole life was an atmosphere of squalor, abuse, drug addiction and suicide.

It was the life I knew. It is why I ended up in some of the situations I ended up in. It was familiar. I am not saying any of those situations was my fault, but it becomes all of what you know.

My father started my brothers on drugs at age 13. I was the oldest of 8, with 4 brothers and 3 sisters. Dad committed suicide at 44, mom died of emphysema at 50. 1 brother overdosed at 41 and another brother committed suicide at age 24 by stepping in front of a train.

After my mom died in 1993, I went into a major depressive episode for a few years. I got divorced from my first husband during the end of that period and am now married to a wonderful man for 18 years.

Where are you now in your healing process?

It has been about a year and a half, since I chose to receive help at a residential rehab called The Meadows. I had gone through many other treatment centers before that dealt with my depression and the symptoms. This was the first place that dealt head on with the trauma, the deep stuff that was there causing so much of the disruption and chaos in my life without my even realizing it.

It was probably the toughest year of my life but also the most rewarding. Coming out of there, I had learned so many tools and so much information on how trauma works on the brain and how it is possible to repair those neuron pathways that have been with me from childhood.

I would not change a thing in my past because it all led to this moment. It led me to be a person who wants to be a beacon of hope for others suffering from these things; someone who forgives, without absolving, for my own benefit. It is the only way forward.

In doing that, it has allowed me to be freer to give back. I am now sharing my story, something that I was not able to do publicly until about six months ago.

I went through so many years of therapy and treatment for depression. One thing that really changed my life is being introduced to the idea of shame and how toxic it is. It helped me to understand why I withdraw, and go into this alone place…because I was filled with shame.

When we understand the shame and understand the path to loving ourselves and coming to the place of forgiving ourselves, it begins the change.

The Meadows is a state of the art facility in Wickenburg, Arizona. They have everything available to treat the trauma. They have survivor workshops, to share your story in a safe environment. They have brain spa where you can go and actually learn how to retrain your brain.

A key element in their training was learning to love yourself, accept what happened and loving ourselves despite it, because I do not think we realize how much we do destruct ourselves.

What words of wisdom would you share with someone just starting down this path?

The first thing is to not worry about the age. Now in my fifties, I felt I was past the point where it would be worth dealing with this. But that is not true. No matter what your age is you need to get into a group, a safe place, anywhere you can safely share your story and start your healing so that you do not feel alone.

Secondly, realize you CAN heal. It does not matter how bad the trauma has been, there are tools and support to help you heal.

Where are you now? Are you feeling joyful? Are you feeling that you have every reason to live and have something to share with the world?

Yes, I am. I am on the board of an organization that works tirelessly to help prevent childhood sexual abuse. I have written my story. I have founded a non-profit organization, I am giving back, and that is what means everything to me. That is what gives what happened to me a purpose.

I also want people to understand that just because you have received help, there are still ups and downs. I have waves. What happened to me will never go away. I walked out of The Meadows thinking I could conquer the world. I still have that in front of me. The difference is that I have learned how to get back up.

My book will be published soon. The telling of my story has been healing for me. I processed it as I wrote.

Organizations Janet Supports:

Show Up for Children: **http://showupforchildren.org/**

SAFE (Sexual Abuse Forever Ended): **www.wersafe.org**

Darkness to Light: **www.darknesstolight.org**

Janet's Video Interview: **https://youtu.be/_gngQvnBcpg**

Chapter 10

Deborah Kinisky

"Try to be a rainbow in someone's cloud."

~ Maya Angelo

"We come to love not by finding the perfect person, but by learning to see an imperfect person perfectly."

~ Sam Keen

"Three things cannot be long hidden: the sun, the moon, and the truth."

~Buddha

"Love is my gift to the world. I fill myself with love, and I sent that love out into the world."

~Dr. Wayne Dyer

By the time I was sixteen years old I was already brutally aware that I was unlovable, unwanted and didn't matter. I was conditioned to be a purple sky survivalist who was growing up a victim of illusions.

I'd been sexually abused by four different men, two of which I was related to and lived in the same house as. I'd survived multiple abuses and traumas and was on a road that led to no good. That was my past.

Today, however I wear many different hats. I'm the executive director of Blue Sky Thrivalist Services, a nurturing mom, loving wife, published author, international photographer and inspirational speaker. I've most recently published Purple Sky Survivalist – Growing Up a Victim of Illusions which portrays how I overcame abuse and addictions, and how I stayed away from an illicit lifestyle, even though I lived neck deep in it.

What are the most positive things you have done to overcome the pain and trauma of your past?

Going back to school at the age of 39 with a grade nine education, thinking I didn't know what I was doing. I successfully completed the mental health rehabilitation course, and through that I was able to self diagnose and through mentoring other students, I learned that I did matter, I was lovable, I was smart and it was time for me to thrive in life and stop simply surviving.

What would you say to someone who is just starting down this path? To someone who is experiencing the pain you and I knew so well and have decided to make a change?

I would say reach out. You are not alone. I would say that there are far more people that have been abused than have not, and that the statistics are not accurate by any stretch. There are many coming out like both of us, and are choosing to thrive. I encourage you to join us.

What is the single best thing you have done for yourself?

It has been putting my story down on paper and sharing it with the world. It was an unleashing of things that needed to be revealed. It was time for the truth to come out because I had been living a lie my whole life. My entire life I had been running and it was time to stop.

I needed to own what happened to me and not be owned by it. It owned me. Purple Sky!

Writing for me has been a key element of change. I am able to express myself without feeling judged because I don't judge my own writing. The only judging I have received by writing my story is positive, amazing and nurturing. So many years I felt so alone and now I KNOW I am not alone.

I am one of millions and as sad and scary as that is, it makes me happy to know that we are starting to speak out about this horrible epidemic. It is a disease and it needs to stop. It bites far deeper than an illness because of the long lasting effects it has on us...including the feelings of unworthiness.

What resources would you recommend?

Connect with nature and things that you are passionate about and people who are passionate about you. Find things that bring us a connection. Maybe it is art. Maybe it is dance. Maybe it is being at the ocean or in the forest. Find what works for you and own it!

One of the things about writing is that we can write in the night when we can't sleep. We can write when others are not available to listen to us, when our counselor is not available, writing is a tool always available to us.

There is no contest with writing. When we are writing, we release it to the world. We release it to the universe and letting the universe deal with it. We have millions of other weight bearers to help us deal with it. When we share it with the world, we are no longer carrying it alone.

There are so many women who are struggling with the same abuses and addictions that we have experienced and they need to know they do not need to do this alone.

There is a cure and it is awareness and speaking out...Share your story.

Deborah's books are:

Purple Sky Survivalist: Growing Up a Victim of Illusions
https://goo.gl/wNMmJn

Her Story: Victim to Victorious, A Memoir
http://amzn.to/2i13MK0

Website: **http://www.deborahkinisky.com/**

Deborah's Video Interview: **https://youtu.be/_o5q1aMEST8**

Chapter 11

Heather Egan

"There is no force more powerful than a woman determined to rise."

~ Mantra Yoga Mag

I have been on the path of sexual recovery for most of my life. I was first sexually molested by a family members' father when I was thirteen years old. I had trusted this man and did not suspect. Shortly afterwards it started with my uncle and lasted until I was 23 when I found my voice. I felt so much shame. It was a lonely journey. I was cloaked in shame. I told my parents, who suggested finding a counselor.

It was suggested to send him a letter to cease or other people would know. He is still in our family and is employed by my family. While he did apologize, he did not know what to say to his wife. My dad helped him concoct a story as to what happened, which really angered my mother.

That's been my story. As an adult, I attracted partners that have that kind of abuse…mostly emotional abuse. It takes a while to gain our voice.

Where are you now in your healing journey?

It is an ongoing evolution. It really is. It is not that I don't get emotional, or that you ever stop fully achieving circumstances that trigger me but I am now on the other side. It is my goal and mission to walk more deeply on this earth because when we have been abused we get so much in our head that we are not connected with anything that is going on below our shoulders, with our heart and what our power center is telling us to do.

So it my mission to walk more grounded in this life, to be more passionate, to walk more deeply and to feel more the beauty that is supposed to be in our life.

We have an underlying grief that hangs on so deeply to our souls. But we do deserve. We do have the choice to live with more joy. We must never feel that this is our lot in our life and this is the only choice we have.

What is the most positive you have done for yourself in this journey?

I think finding the joy that is so rightfully my birthright and realizing that there is more depth to life.

I've started my own small business being of service to women who have been sexually abused. It is not counseling, it is not coaching, it is mentoring. It is dealing with the arts rather than talking.

We can talk so much that we do not realize what has been stored in our bodies. Why do we attract either in personal relationships or even work relationships the people we do?

The art part of it, expressing through dance, song, poetry, musical instrument, drawing…these things get the body open to releasing the things that need to dissolved.

How did you figure out these modalities for healing?

I worked with children for 27 years and it was very much play based and what the interest of the child was at the time. It was not a strict curriculum. When you really delve into what you enjoy, that's when the healing self expression can take place.

As a child I played the piano and played instruments over the years.

I started working with an intuitive artist several years ago. It was interesting to me to dance, which I had never done. Dance for me was awkward, especially in high school, so I never responded to it. Now, I have learned how the body can take over and have movement of its' own.

The same goes for drawing. You do not have to be Picasso. Mine drawings are very simple, they are very much stick figures and symbols but it gets me connected to what I need to let go of.

What words of wisdom would you give to someone just starting on this journey?

Start simple. Put one step in front of the other. If that is talking to a friend, seeing a therapist, finding a community perhaps in a Facebook group, do it. Surround yourself with support.

There is so much out there to take advantage of, there is much more than there used to be. Be gentle and loving with yourself because it will be many forward steps. Be diligent because there will be trigger points that will make you feel like your going backwards instead of forward.

I read Courage to Heal and it was huge for me and I still go back to that, especially as I mentor my clients.

If you have a partner, they have a book for partners as well.

Another book that really helped me was "The Journey from Abandonment to Healing." That one gets into relationship with your inner child and being a mother to yourself.

It is a different world now. Very unlike the time our grandmother's lived and this was unspeakable.

Website: **www.sacredfeminine.ca**

Facebook business page

https://www.facebook.com/Sacred-Feminine-empowered-abuse-recovery-753218718149046/

Heather's Video Interview: **https://youtu.be/i7vmuOnch7E**

Courage to Heal: **http://amzn.to/2hhH38Q**

Journey from Abandonment to Healing: **http://amzn.to/2i0NLnG**

Chapter 12

Brenda Hammon

"It is what it is. Move forward or stay behind. Your choice."

~Brenda Hammon

I grew up in rural Alberta, Canada. My parents had moved there in the 1950's and were homesteaders, homesteaders were people that bought raw land and had to clear so many acres per year and put into production according to the Homesteader Rule set out by the government. We did not have any other family around as it was just my family that moved there. I came along several years later after their arrival into this rugged country.

My abuse started when I was five years old by a family friend, he was Dad's farmhand. He was the son of a long time family friend that Dad had helped out when they also had moved up north. The abuse from the farm hand had continued throughout the summer of my fifth year and then it escalated when both the farmhand and a family member that raped me. It ended right after that, but the damage was done.

The farmhand's sexual and mental abuse had shattered and terrified me. I was always afraid that he would kill my family as he threatened to if I ever told anyone what he was doing to me. My whole life altered and shifted yet again when my family member also became involved, it crushed me and nearly destroyed my soul. Now I could not trust anyone. Before, I could at least trust someone, but when that happened, I lost all trust in everyone.

When the farmhand was abusing me I would ran out into the bush and hide, nobody knew where I was. But after the family member became involved then I literally started to run for my life. I ran away from home every day, leaving first thing in the morning and arriving home at the end of the day. Again no one knew where I went every day.

I look at my five year old granddaughter now, and I am in shock. I can hardly imagine her living the way I had too, because I was still a baby and I was surviving on my own. I became a tough kid because I had to be. I lived inside the family unit but yet I lived on the outside, I was always looking through the screen at everybody else, watching them. I was in the fear and flight mode, that mode stayed with me for decades.

Yes, my parents fed and clothed me, but to me, that was the extent of it. My survival became my norm. I did not trust anyone. This lack of trust affected my relationships with boys and even with my female friends. Trust became such a huge determining factor for me. If I did not trust you, then I did not need you in my life, or anywhere close to me.

It became almost like unbalanced weigh scale, 100% on one side, and 0% on the other side. It was crazy, and all of my relationships suffered. My first marriage was a huge disaster. I thought he would protect me as he promised but he turned out to be a sex addict with a few other problems.

We seem to attract that which we know. I didn't know any better, I was trying to make correct decisions without the necessary skills to do that because of the sexual and mental abuse.

I certainly felt like I was putting out 'abuse me' vibes. I think I had a neon sign on my forehead that flashed "Abuse Me." This mentality seems to become ingrained in me.

It took me over 40 years to figure it out. That is a long time to finally stand up and say NO. I finally knew I had to make a change!

For my whole life I ran and I could run really well. Victims of abuse do that and we do it well. The words that the abusers have said to you about your value in life, stick to you like mud. It is hard to scrape this off because it has been dried on, and caked on for so long, layer after layer. It is engrained in you. Scrapping off the mud from my abusers and learning how to live past the abuse, now that has been a challenge.

Where are now on your healing journey?
I am actually really good. I've done my journey but I know my journey is not over. I used to feel that "oh I have done my therapy, and I am good." Ha! I know that I have what I call M.E.D. That is a mental and emotional disability. It is not PTSD. You cannot see it. It is from my abusers and comes up and rears its' ugly head every once in a while.

I know I have to live with that. There are triggers for me…mine is if someone tells me I am not looking after my horse properly. If I could put shoes and fur coats on all of my horses I would.

There are triggers and those triggers are about trust. I get really defensive. A person just has to do one little thing to destroy my trust in them and getting the trust back takes forever. I have to realize that their actions are about them and not about me. I just have to recognize that and not get bogged down with it all.

I've done many forms of therapy and recently I've also done cellular release. I've done so much to get it out of my brain and out of my heart. I know it will always be a memory, but now it is a distant memory. The cellular release therapy was to help me to get it out of my body. That was another journey the needed to be done and I am glad that I did it. If there is anything else that rears its' ugly little head, then I will do what it takes to remove it. I know that those memories will always be there, it is a part of who I am.

Out of all the positive things you have done to be well and happy, which do you feel has had the most impact?
Seeking help for the first time and actually having someone say: "Oh my God, something else is going on with this woman, now what is it?"

When I went to get help, it was because my ex-husband had died and I was blamed for his death. With all of the fall-out from that, I went to my doctor and I told her that I thought I was going crazy.

Then I told her what was going on so she recommended I go see this amazing therapist.

She was a grief counselor and it did not take her long to figure out there was more going on than what she was seeing on the surface. She cracked open my Pandora's Box, but I was not willing to look at it. I thought to myself, I know about the abuse, that it was in my past, let's move past that.

I had a rude awakening. Yes, it was in the past, but unless we deal with it, you do not move forward.

For those just starting out on their own healing journey what would you say to them?

Do not be afraid. It is going to get tough. If you need to take a break, then take a break. It is ok. But do not be afraid, because what is at the end of the tunnel is something that you have never imagined in your whole life, that your life could be this good. It is powerful and inspiring. You have to walk through hell to get there. Frankly, you have already been through hell, now you are just going back through the gates and leave the hell behind.

The fear of what you will go through when you are going through the healing process is nowhere near as bad as what you have been through already. For me, I had been in hell for such a long time, and when I had to walk out of it, it was like walking the gauntlet. But I could see those gates; I was determined to walk out through those gates and leave the past in the past where it belonged instead of hanging on to me like a cling-on, dragging me down wherever I went.

Brenda, I read the first book you wrote, "I Can't Hear the Birds Anymore," and now the second book, "I AM". There is quite a contrast between the two books, lots of healing. Tell us about your journey in writing these two books.

When I wrote the first book, it was written from the five year old child's point of view. How she felt. Because it was written from a five year olds view, it is a tougher read, but it a real read. The decisions that child made from a five year old, to a ten year old, a fifteen year old, a twenty year old, even from a twenty-five year old were all affected by what happened to her and not dealing with it. Near the end of the book it talks about the healing and dealing with it. It is a pretty strong but necessary book. It is a necessary book, because sometimes things get sugar coated. It is raw, it is vulnerable and it is real.

The second book "I AM" is more written from my perspective as a woman. My journey. It started off not going through the healing yet and dealing with things, realizing that my life has to be better than this. It came from knowing that I can no longer be a piñata for abusers. There has to be something else in my life. It is a way different journey as a woman than it was as a child. This book is very strong and powerful and gives the message that if I can go through it and if I can survive it, then anybody can survive it.

Writing my book brought a lot of healing. You must get it out of your heart and out of your brain and put it on paper. Otherwise it just rolls around in there and causes a lot of damage. The minute you start writing it down it takes it out of your body.

Even if you do not share it, it gets it out. Perhaps you do not want to share it because of your family. Writing is a phenomenal healing tool. When you write it, you write a new story for yourself.

If you do share it, be aware of the issues that can come to the fore because of the family. A family has a difficult time dealing with it. Often they do not rally behind the victim, they rally around the abuser. Telling your family can be the most difficult part.

When I wrote my first book, my body had an emotional charge and it reacted like I was still in the trauma. I got sick, and had infections. That is when I went and got cellular release. Because I had addressed that issue, I did not have those issues for my second book.

What do you believe is the key factor that causes people to NOT go through the process?

Fear and shame. Those are the two biggest things. You have been told not to tell, you are terrified to tell. The fear of telling and fear of what

71

others will think of you along with the shame because we always tend to think it was our fault.

Often the family will turn against you because they do not want it brought it out in the open. Often they do not see you as a whole person. They often do not want to face the responsibility that they hold for not protecting you. It is easier to put shame on the victim than on themselves.

You've told us about your books, you mentioned a workbook that you have written. Tell us about it.

The workbook is an interactive book called, "I AM: Your Journey of Self Discovery.

It starts out talking about making changes in your life. If you feel like you are in a wash machine and the load is unbalanced, then it is time to find out why.

There are exercises in there to help you clear your mind and relax and start to think about who you truly are inside. It will help you open up your memories. If there is something in there that needs to be dealt with, whether it is the patterns of your life or something about the abuse or something else, each segment has a section where you will explore and then color the corresponding design.

The first one starts off with your soul. Then it goes into cocoons and butterflies. Each one is about courage, determination, compassion…for yourself…not for anyone else. It is about your own journey of seeing you through new eyes.

You must have happiness after abuse. We have a choice. My story is no less tragic than others. I do not hold a corner on the market. You can take back your life and live the life you are meant to live.

My life is what it is, I can let the past destroy me or I can conquer it and step into the life I WANT.

Brenda's Books:

I Can't Hear the Birds Anymore: **http://amzn.to/2iALDQl**

I AM: Kicking Down the Walls of Silence About Sexual and Mental Abuse: **http://amzn.to/2iAPNba**

Brenda's Workbook:
http://www.spiritcreekpublishing.com/booksproducts.html

Brenda's Video Interview: **https://youtu.be/GWKRX4n0fPQ**

Chapter 13

Edna J. White

"Our deepest fear is not that we are inadequate. Our deepest fear is that we are powerful beyond measure. It is our Light, not our Darkness, that most frightens us."

~ Marianne Williamson

My abuse stay abuse started at age five and continued until I was 15 at the hands of my stepfather, then later by a series of men introduced to my life as family. It was devastating to my self esteem. I was nervous with all men, including my uncles and cousins. Most of the time, I was alone in my room. I avoided being alone with people, especially me.

As I got older, I identified with men by flirting, because I thought that was normal. I wanted to be liked. The sexual abuse over time from men who were supposed to create a safe environment for me, devalued me and as I entered the 'tween-age years, I became so confused. I went from hating men to doing everything in my power to get their attention.

As I became a teenager I became promiscuous and being with men was just a catalyst to my control over them. I didn't stay in relationships long, only to my control. If it was not on my terms…done!

As an adult, I hadn't learned anything about relationships. My experience in my family was damaged, my self-esteem was lower than mud in the street and my self-worth was zero. I had believed a lie that I "was only here to please my perpetrator." It limited all my relationships and totally stopped my emotional growth at the age of 5 years old. Every experience would be seen through an adults eyes but processed from and 5-year olds perception.

I had lists of what I expected out of even platonic relationships, and the minute I saw something that did not measure up, they were no longer friends. Holding on to such pain and familiar charades, I had become a professional liar. Not intentionally, but because it was ingrained in me to keep the secret. Everything was a lie.

It was the year that I was 18 years old. I had stayed out all night at a friend's house and I had taken my 12 month old child with me. This day I realized I was inclined to suicide. I skipped right over alcohol and went to really hard drugs. I felt an overwhelming cloud over me that pulled me into a depressive state. I wanted to die. And be induced by drugs, I took my child with me. I literally sat on the train tracks and waited for the train to come. But it never did. I sat there until after nightfall. That was my miracle that day. As I walked home with a tear streaked face, it would be just 24 hours more that the magic would continue.

The next day as I rode the bus, still crying and holding my son, a woman who sat diagonally across from me pulled the bell to get off. She, like others saw me crying. As she walked past me she gently touched my shoulder and gave me a card, whispering, "It is going to be alright." The card was to a psychiatrist. That was my first start to healing.

Right after that, I was still longing for change, for healing of this core feeling that I wasn't complete. I started going to church. It wasn't that I didn't know God, because I remember writing letters to him asking him to rescue me when I was little. I needed peace. But that peace was short lived.

As I started getting involved in church, my family and the perpetrator followed, so that they could keep me from telling the secret. My time at this church was fulfilling yet tragic. Not only had I been raped in my home, my self-worth was questioned yet again. I was spiritually raped at the church. The clergy did not believe enough in me to create a place of healing. I was put on the back burner yet again. Once again, my perpetrator was authority figures.

Where are you now on your healing journey?

My healing journey took me many years of support groups, challenging myself, reading to educate myself and learning all about the real me. I am doing really well. I finally learned that I don't have to be simply a survivor, I can recover.

I learned to forgive myself because I felt like maybe I liked the act of abuse against me. I had to realize that I did not understand and know what was normal and my feelings and actions were not my fault. Forgiveness is what I needed to do for myself. Until I learned to forgive myself, my progress of healing and relating to others was slow.

I suffered financially as an adult, relating to what I suffered as a child. You see, my stepfather gave me money as a reward when we molested me. I hated it. When he gave it to me, I washed it with soap and water. Then, I would iron it and put it away under the bed and never use it. I refused to touch it, and hated that money!

It took me a good while to understand my aversion to money as an adult. For so long, I could not hold money. When I finally figured where this aversion came from, I learned that I had to forgive myself even about accepting the money.

Money was not the reason why I am going through this. I had to go through the process of learning why I did what I do and I learned eventually to get rid of things like anger, hatred, attitudes, anguish and fear. In order for me to move on and be happy, I had to get rid of what no longer served me.

This process is very much like peeling an onion. Just because I understood that lack of me not forgiving myself was affecting me. There will be triggers and it takes diligence to understand and work through the process.

At one point, when I began writing about my experiences, my self-esteem that had me write a complete manuscript, only to later forget all about it and leave it stored away in archives. Until one day, I received an email alert that I had documents stored in the cloud. I was reintroduced to my story, my book, written some three years prior.

It was shocking to me as I read it, that such beautiful words came from someone like me. I cried. The only way that I can explain it is that God had to take me through a journey within myself to know myself. He had to prepare me to release the book. All I heard was God saying, "It is time."

I was afraid of how others would feel about me. I was afraid of friends not accepting me.

Now that I have published my story, I feel freer than a bird! I have enough self-worth and self-esteem to leave a 15 year real estate career to coach other that have experienced sexual trauma to recovery.

What words of wisdom would you share with those just starting out on their healing journey?

Not everyone is the same. The way you heal is the way you heal. Do not compare yourself to others. You will get it. It is ok to feel what you feel when you feel it. You have a right to get mad, get angry and cry. Realize that choosing to love yourself past the pain and tough memories will help you in all relationships, issues and conflicts.

Read books and fill your mind with as much positive as possible.

Many of us lost so much of what was normal as children. We had to keep secrets for a very long time, and all the important things that would prepare us for adulthood was stripped from us. Know that you are not alone and seek the help that you need. Never give up on your efforts to heal.

Know that it may take a search of many different therapists before you find one that works for you.

You will have stages of healing and what you feel is alright. You can recover!

Edna's Video Interview: **https://youtu.be/ITk-6y1PTHM**

Edna's book: "Stuff - Giving Voice to the Secret"
http://amzn.to/2jbpY2j

Chapter 14

Shannon Gardner

"Becoming a Victim is not a choice. Becoming a survivor is."

~ Juan Quotes

Shannon born in Nebraska and grew up in Iowa and Illinois. She has been an Arizona resident for over 30 years, has a 24 year old son and five year old grandson and has been married to her current husband for close to three years. She has had her current business for two years.

When I was 5, I was sexually abused by my caregiver while my mom worked 2 jobs. It happened multiple times. It affected me so much that every time someone would go to change my clothes or bath me, I would think they were going to abuse me. I became very untrusting of everyone.

It has affected my life in so many ways. I have been married 4 times because of it. The first 3 did not understand what I was feeling, but my current husband is so understanding and supportive.

This trauma has caused me to have major anxiety, trust issues and sleepless nights.

I was a sophomore in high school when my mom and I were watching an after school special about sexual abuse. It was so hard for me to sit and watch it without my mom knowing. I decided to tell her what happened to me.

In my mind by telling her things would get better. Of course the questions came, why didn't I tell her? I had no answers, except to say that I did not want to get in trouble, and that I thought it was my fault, I did something wrong.

Fast forward, I married my first husband. It lasted only a year. I married my second husband and it lasted only two years and he was unfaithful to me because I could not be intimate because of my trauma. He did not understand that and did not accept that, so went elsewhere.

My third husband, I was married to for fifteen years. He did not understand, so we fought continuously. It was a big argument with us all of the time. His words were that I needed to go get help, go get counseling. We all know that is not a fix. Counseling might have helped, but it needs to start with support in a relationship. He needed to be supportive. He could not be, so that marriage did not work out.

I am married now to my fourth husband, he is very understanding and supportive. If I have a bad day, and am not feeling happy and am in that depressed mode, he cares and does not push. He is a wonderful man.

I joined Younique, and within a year of joining they started the Younique Foundation. It is a retreat for women that had been sexually abused before the age of eighteen. I went to the four day retreat in the mountains of Utah.

We did journaling, we art journaled, we did yoga, had therapy, we drummed, we did so much. It was fantastic. We had a chef that cooked great food for us.

We were taught that we are not alone and it was not our fault; that we had not asked for this to happen to us. We were taught that we are survivors and warriors and have a great support group.

Before the retreat, I did a video with Younique where I told about my story for the first time. That is when the world found out what happened to me. I struggled with that because I wrestled with whether

I wanted my son to know about what happened to me. It was tough, but I felt that if he does not know, he would not know what happened and would not understand me. It was tough for about a week after I released it.

After I released it, I had so many women reach out to me and some were really close friends, and I would not have known they had gone through the same thing. That is where I opened up and where my healing began.

I'm working on myself so that I can help others. I'm still not very trusting, but I'm working through the anxiety.

What words of wisdom would you share with someone who has decided to take that step to begin their healing journey?

To know that this was not their fault and they are not just a survivor, they are a warrior. Don't let the person who did this, win.

Find someone they can really trust and open up to if they need to talk, especially during those tough days. This needs to be someone who will not judge them, who will listen and not tell them that they need to just get over it.

Often we don't want the lecture...we just need someone to listen. There will be times that something that will happen that will open it up.

What resources did you tap into that helped you are your healing journey?

Reclaim Hope is a workbook they gave us.

If we are going through a tough day, be sure to journal. Write about the senses that are involved. Sights, smells, things you hear, use art when you journal. Do it daily so you can associate what the trigger points are and see the patterns that set you off.

Do what you need to help take your mind away from the pain and focus on happy thing.

Younique Foundation: **http://youniquefoundation.org/**

Reclaim Hope: **http://youniquefoundation.org/hope/**

Shannon's Video Interview: **https://youtu.be/w66e1Rs7FEw**

Chapter 15

Diana Dunham

"Everything happens for a reason."

~ Diana Dunham

Diana Dunham is a 58 year old mother of two, a grandmother of three. She's been married to her second husband going on 32 years, and it's because of her husband's strength that she was able to get through what she experienced.

I was maybe eight or nine when it began, and it was my father that abused me. It stopped when I was about 13, and I always thought it was just because I said it had to stop, but after I started getting counseling, and the counselor was the one that helped me realize that is that the reason he stopped was because he had been abusing my older sister as well. She had told my mother, so he then decided to stop.

Well, thankfully it stopped, but it also had its repercussions. It did. I lived with that all my life and it wasn't until I dealt with it, it was always in the background. I've always had a relationship with my father, but it wasn't until I had my own daughter and she then became five, that I realized that I had to protect her.

I was going to a counselor, my husband's a Vietnam veteran, and I was going to this counselor because we were having marriage problems because of his PTSD, and she picked right up on it that that's...I probably had some issues.

We delved into it. I spent maybe eight months with the counselor, and at the time, I disassociated myself with my family. My grandmother passed away and I wasn't able to go to the funeral.

I think my mother sort of knew maybe what was going on, but nobody wanted to broach it.

Then the counselor finally said, "You've hit a plateau. You have to talk to your mother so she knows why," so I did, and my mother...the biggest fear was would she believe me after all these years, and she did.

Did it happen to your sister, too?

Yes. My elder sister, and unfortunately has nothing to do with our family. She's disassociated herself from the family. My sister is a social worker, and I had talked to her, and my father tried with her too.

She thought because she told dad no, that's why he stopped. That's not why. He stopped because he was afraid of being caught.

Then I talked with my mother, and she believed me, and we cried. She went home and she confronted my father, and shortly thereafter we found out that he had cancer. We confronted him in September, found out he had cancer in December, and he died the following July. His biggest fear to my mother was on his deathbed, was being forgiven, and he was.

Forgiveness is something that we do for ourselves. Yes, we do it for the others too, but it's largely for ourselves, because that's the only way we're going to heal.

Where are you now on your healing path?

Because he passed away, that added a lot of closure. I didn't have to worry anymore. The counselor was great. I don't go to counseling anymore. My husband, like I said, he stood behind me 100%. Very few people know. I know, he knows, my sister knows. My kids don't need to know. That was their grandfather, so now I just want to give back and help people, so that's where I'm at.

Would you say that the counseling was the most positive thing that you have done for yourself?

Yes. The counseling, and the fact that I was able to tell my mother, and that she believed me. Also, that we continued to have a very close relationship until she passed away in 2001.

That's beautiful. That helped with the entire healing process didn't it? You took that step, of speaking up and that took a lot of courage. That's something that some of us come by early, and some of us don't speak until we are much older. I suspect many have gone to the grave with their deep dark secret.

Yes, it did take courage. Thank you for acknowledging that! I never blamed myself. I knew it wasn't right, and I know I wasn't the reason. I have a very, very strong faith, and I think that's one of the reasons that I survived as I did, because I knew that that didn't define who I was. I think it made me a stronger person, because I did survive it. At the time, when I disassociated myself from my family, I have two other brothers, and my youngest brother, he didn't really say much of anything, but I got a very scathing letter from my one younger brother. I had had a hysterectomy. They blamed it on the hysterectomy. I was going off on the deep end.

I could've retorted. I could've, but I didn't want to. I didn't want them to think poorly of their father, and same thing with my kids. I don't want my kids ... My son was very, very close to his grandfather, and I don't want him to be tainted by that. I want him to have the memories that he had. My mother, I remember so we got the counseling, and the counselor said, "You know, your mother has to come in," and mom did. My mother was a survivor of World War II in Berlin, so I'm sure there were a lot of horrific things there. My father, he came to the counseling, and he apologized.

In his mind, he thought, "Your mother wasn't that loving," so it's ... Even though he apologized, I never really felt like he really, truly understood.

After my dad died, my mother and I had further conversations, and even in her mind, she tried to rectify ... Like, "I think your father had been abused as a child." That doesn't make it right. I'm his child. He shouldn't have.

As I said with my older sister, she had confronted my mother when she was 18. My mother didn't believe her. My mother called her a liar, and we really never had much of a relationship with her. I think she hooked up with the wrong guy. He probably does drugs. She's an abused, battered wife. When my dad died, she did come to the funeral. I thought she and my mom would rekindle, but they didn't. Then when my mom died, she didn't come to the funeral.

That's very typical. If the pain and the issues have not been confronted and dealt with, usually there's such isolation. It's happened in my family as well.

I reached out to her, and I do believe I had told her of my struggles, and told her that I was here for her if she wanted to, and she never did.

What would be your words of advice to somebody starting out on the healing?

My advice would be find someone, anyone that you can talk to that you trust, that believes in you, and that can help you with the healing. That may not be the very first person. I went through three counselors before I found the right person, so don't feel that because one or two people don't understand that the third or the fourth person won't. You need to find that person that you can connect with. If religion is in your life, seek out religious healers. That is great.

There are so many self-help books out there. One of the books that my counselor had given me to read was a book that Suzanne Somers had written. It was full of short stories.

They were just short stories, but that helps us know that we are not alone.

Journal. Journaling is awesome. You write the stuff down, because the more you write it down, the more, not so much that you remember, the more it empowers you,

Because I was able to talk about this, that I was able to survive this. Just know that it's not you. You didn't cause this. You didn't ask for it. You didn't cause it. It's nothing that you did. It's the other person that is sick, is twisted, and needs help.

Thank you Diana, for sharing those wonderful words. I've come to believe and really understand the healing power of story by writing our story, whether we ever publish it, no matter what we do with it, mere writing of it changes us because in the process we write a new story.

We do, and whether you express it in poetry, or song, or anything, just get your feelings out. I mean, I used to talk to my dog, because I had a little dog. Mine happened in the barn, and the dog would be out there, and I would talk to the dog.

You have to talk to somebody. You have to talk to somebody. That would be my words. Yep. You have to talk to somebody.

Diana's Video Interview: **https://youtu.be/aIZJ_5kncZs**

Chapter 16

Amanda Hollis-Thompson

"Even though you may want to move forward in your life, you may have one foot on the brakes. In order to be free, we must learn how to let go. Release the hurt. Release the fear. Refuse to entertain your old pain. The energy it takes to hang onto the past is holding you back from a new life. What is it you would let go of today?"

~ Mary Manin Morrissey

It's hard to say exactly when sexual abuse began for me. It peppers many of my memories from childhood starting at a very young age from various people. Though, none of those memories are what turned my world completely upside down and shook me to my core.

My world changed at 14 years of age, I lived in Naples, Florida and was in the 9th grade. You can say I was a pretty typical teenager in that I like to be involved in normal teenager things like going to the mall, talking on the phone, and spending time with my friends. One evening, one of my friends and I decided to walk to the mall from her house. It was super hot and muggy out, so one of her neighbors-Steve (and family friend) was more than happy to take us with but one stipulation…he wanted to make a few stops of his own. My friend trusted this man so it sounded like a good plan to me.

After running a few errands (including a liquor store), I thought we were on our way to the mall. However, Steve decided to turn off course and go a different route. Instead, he took us to a very remote, overgrown area and proceeded to try and get me to drink some vodka he had bought. I had just a few sips before he suggested that he and I go on a walk to talk about birthday ideas for my friend.

Once we were a decent ways back into the wooded area, I quickly learned that he didn't want to talk to me at all! He wanted to have sex with me. In spite of me telling him no, he physically kept pulling my shorts down and untying the sides, until he had my shorts down. Before I knew it, he had me down on the ground and was inside me as I was crying and pleading for him to stop. After he was done, he stood me up and patted me on the butt saying "see, it wasn't that bad, was it? I told you, you would like it." Physically I was okay. But, I felt like I was dying inside.

I didn't tell my friend what had happened that night out of embarrassment. I thought maybe I had done something to encourage him. I thought that maybe I shouldn't have worn the short shorts I had on. I didn't know how to feel about anything that had happened, outside of just feeling dirty, gross, and violated.

In truth, I don't think I fully understood that I was raped until about 6 months later when I received a phone call. I'll never forget that phone call. My mom called me, while I was visiting family in Oklahoma, and asking what Steve had done to me. She didn't ask me "if" something had happened...She asked me what had happened.

I had kept it all bottled up inside for so long that I cried and broke down telling her where she could find my sealed journal entry in my room explaining the night of the events. She collected my journal entry to give to the police and proceeded to tell me that Steve had also raped my friend on a different night. My friend had come forward saying that she thought I had possibly been raped as well.

From there, I was immediately flown back to Naples. It was way too late to undergo any medical testing to see if my story was accurate. However, I was not allowed to have any contact with my friend before I could be questioned in detail by the police. While Steve sat in jail under the accusations from my friend, he also awaited my testimony and any proof I could produce to add to the charges. Based on my accounts of the event, my journal entry, and my ability to take the police officer back to the location of my rape; it appeared Steve would be booked on charges of two accounts of statutory rape and sentenced to quite a few years in prison. However, Steve never made it to prison because he hung himself with his bed sheets before he could ever even go to trial.

I wish this is where I could say that I felt that justice was served. But at an immature 14 years of age, I felt more like a murderer. He left behind a wife, and 3 or 4 small children and I was indirectly responsible for it. It took a long time to get past that. I was so upset that his children wouldn't have a father that I wished I had just stayed silent, for many years. I was without my father from actions not of my own when I was young. I felt responsible for depriving these kids of theirs. Sometimes I think Steve's suicide actually stayed with me longer than the rape. After all, I was a child that grew up with the familiarity of sexual abuse anyway.

Where are you now on your healing journey?
Now, I am in much healthier mental place.

After years of confusion, guilt, and shame, I can now say I am much better. I had allowed this event to define who I was for entirely too long. I firmly believe that my pushing it down and not dealing with it even contributed to the demise of an 18 year long marriage.

I spent years trying to figure out who I was and why I felt so out of place. I was so wrapped up in the past that it began to cloud my judgment and reality. I even remember telling my ex-husband that I felt like I needed some major help and that I felt crazy and unstable but I didn't know why. I literally felt like I was self-destructing and couldn't stop myself from doing it. Turns out, I wasn't crazy, or unstable. Though, I did require help with figuring out how to move past my rape. All I had done was shove it down inside and it was surfacing at a rate faster than I knew how to deal with.

Now, while I may still have occasional flash-backs and bad dreams, I am no longer paralyzed by my past. I no longer hold myself to blame for the death of the man who raped me. I am able to talk about it much easier as well. I'll never truly understand why it happened to me.

But I don't have to. His decision to violate me isn't mine to understand. It happened and that's all there is to it. I cannot let it shape and define me any longer. I will say that when I do write about it or talk about it, there are still some after effects. I have to admit that it does get to me sometimes. That, and there are occasional trigger words that leave me feeling breathless and helpless all over again. But, I gently remind myself that I am not that defenseless little girl anymore and that I have moved past this. In short, I'm still a work in progress.

What has been the most positive thing you have done for yourself to overcome the trauma of your past?

The most positive thing I have done for myself is to decide to move past it and to live in the present. I have come to a place where I no longer require having the whys answered.

I also forgave myself for not being "smart" enough to see through his lies and trickery, and for not screaming NO at the top of my lungs that night. I also had to forgive myself for keeping it a secret from even my friend, who then became his next victim.

Another thing I have done that has proven immensely helpful to me is to start my own company called Delightfully Vixen with my boyfriend. In my business, I am a professional bra-fitter, lingerie consultant and intimacy coach/sex educator.

The best part about this business is that it has opened up the doors for me to better assist other women who have hang-ups with intimacy and sex like I did.

Whereas, the topic of sex and intimacy (or anything surrounding it) once scared me as equally as it intrigued me, I now fully embrace the topic.

I have grown away from that embarrassed little girl into a woman who has made a conscious decision to move up and onward.

What words of wisdom can you offer to those who have just begun their own journey of healing?

To anyone just starting out on the journey of healing from any type of sexual trauma, I say do what feels right for you as long as you are making forward progression.

There is no one path that is the answer for all of us. I attempted a support group when I was 19 years old and quickly realized that it wasn't for me. Perhaps it was just the wrong group and I should have tried another one, but I didn't feel better rehashing my experiences week after week. It made it feel like it was always just yesterday that the rape happened.

I felt better, and was able to process through more, by attending a journaling workshop where I was able to write about my experiences and then given the tools to reshape my thoughts into productive venues. I grew more by learning to understand that the experience did not define me as a person, my thoughts did.

What resources can you recommend to those just beginning on their journey of healing?

Some of the resources I used proved to be more beneficial than others. I would say the best resource available to me was just an old fashioned spiral and a pen. I found it immensely beneficial to journal my feelings.

Then, as I grew older and began college, I enrolled in psychology classes which I am sure helped me to find some of my own path through learning the various methods of dealing with life situations.

Other resources that proved beneficial to me were self-help books focused on topics such as PTSD, Sexual Abuse such as "The Wounded Heart - Hope for Adult Victims of Childhood Sexual Abuse" by Dr. Dan B. Allender, and specific journaling instruction books and theories such as "The Way of the Journal."

"The Wounded Heart - Hope for Adult Victims of Childhood Sexual Abuse" by Dr. Dan B. Allender **http://amzn.to/2jbpzNz**

"The Way of the Journal:" by Kathleen Adams
http://amzn.to/2iWuHoT

Amanda's Video Interview: **https://youtu.be/Ozx0VD9utW8**

Chapter 17

Nikki Dubose

I'm a former model turned author, speaker and mental health advocate. My debut memoir that I have just written is called "Washed Away from Darkness to Light." It covers life through my eyes from age two through age 27. I am 31 now.

I have been in recovery from a variety of mental health issues which started when I was a witness to domestic violence in my home. I was also myself physically, sexually, verbally and emotionally abused.

That spawned a very long 17 year battle with eating disorders and other co-occurring disorders, such as depression, and psychosis, which I was officially diagnosed with last year.

For all the years I was dealing with that, I didn't know what it was. My other issue was sexual addictions. I've been a workaholic. I think is really important to come forward about this because in America a lot of Americans are workaholics and think that's okay.

Where are you now in your healing journey?

Well, thank God, I do give him all the credit. I have been sober from alcohol and drugs for the past five years and free from my eating disorder. I have been in strong recovery from that for the past three and a half years. Of course, because I've dealt with so many different issues, I wouldn't say I struggle, but I am faced with challenges all across the board.

I thank God. I give him all the credit, I really do. I am a firm believer in the 12 steps and that it's really helped me, so I have been free from alcohol and drugs, sober, for the past five years. I have been going strong and free from my eating disorder or the past three and a half years.

It's huge, but it is one day at a time, and sometimes one moment at a time. It is really important that I say this, because even though I know I am getting better, there are moments or triggers that affect me. I will acknowledge that mental illnesses can be a factor. For me, where drugs and the alcohol were concerned, it was very environmental.

I'll hear some type of music that will play and it will trigger me. I have learned to watchful for the things, the triggers that are not good for me. I've definitely had to change my lifestyle completely. I can't hang out with certain types of people that are like my old self because it's like that, you know? I'm not a perfect person. I just have to make the choice everyday to be a better person.

I would say that I do struggle with certain things more than others. I feel that sexual addiction is a result of trauma from childhood. When we're not born into a naturally healthy environment, it changes us, and so it's harder as adults to say that's okay. There's no shame in that.

What would you think the most healing thing that you have done to heal from the trauma of the past?

A healthy identity is so important to me. I didn't know who I was at all. My identity was, I would say, stolen from me. Not having that healthy childhood, I looked for all different ways to shape my identity. For me personally, it was gaining a spiritual identity that has greatly helped me. If it weren't for that, I don't know where I would be right now. Again, I'm not saying that I'm some "holier than thou" person because I'm completely the opposite in that.

I'm very, very human and I struggle. I want to make it very clear that I struggle every, single day and I make a million mistakes. I definitely don't look down on myself when I make a mistake. I understand that I have a Heavenly Father who loves and accepts me, and I think that's what helps keep me from sliding back into the eating disorder and the drugs and alcohol. It helps me say "its' okay," and continue moving forward. I know that I'm God's child. It gives me a lot of real confidence, whereas before, my confidence was rooted in all of the wrong things.

All of the superficial things, this false glamour and things like that, in my work and in my modeling career that never ended up well, because those things can be taken from us very, very quickly.

I started working in television first. I started working in modeling when I was 16 and then was kind of bullied and fat shamed, so then I got out of that. Later I tried to push my way into the entertainment business and started working in television and then had a real professional career in modeling for a long time. It greatly shaped me, because I didn't have any self esteem, and all the other mental health issues that I had.

I allowed my work and, the way that other people perceived me as, to become my identity. That was a disaster, because when you combine that with mental health issues and addictions and things like that it is a recipe for disaster. That is why so many times in the entertainment business we hear so-and-so committed suicide or so-and-so died of an overdose.

I was headed that way because I had no guidance and no love for myself. Leaving that business and going through recovery, it was the greatest gift ever.

Not to put anyone down. I'm working right now to help change the modeling industry because it needs to be a regulated industry. We want to change laws, create laws. It's not to put anyone down or to expose anyone in that sort of way, it's just that it can benefit from changes because there are a lot of minors working that business. In no industry is it okay for someone to be abused, exploited or raped.

What words of wisdom would you care to share with our readers, if somebody was starting on this path of change and making the choice that it's time to take action to start healing and eventually to be thriving in their lives?

The number one most important thing I would say is that you are worth all the love in the world and if you are feeling like you need to reach out for help that's great because you're self-aware and that's very important.

A lot of people aren't self-aware, so give yourself a big pat on the back. Don't be harsh on yourself.

Just reach out because there is always someone who is willing to help you, and who wants to and is ready to help you. Isolation is one of the biggest friends of mental illness but it's an illusion. It's not real.

Reach out, fight.

Fight all the voices that tell you not to reach out. You will find that the moment that you do reach out, you are going to be received with love and kindness and support.

Are there specific resources, is there a book you read, some type of organization that you've acquainted with that you recommend?

There are so many. If you go to my website **www.nikkidubose.com**, and click on 'resources', I have an entire list of resources from everything from eating disorders to trauma to suicide prevention.

First of all, if you are experiencing domestic violence, please call 911 immediately.

If you are a survivor of child sexual abuse, you can visit **http://www.PeacefulHeartsFoundation.org**. I work with this organization.

If you are struggling with an eating disorder I recommend you call the National Eating Disorders Association Hotline. They also have a confidential click-to-chat.

Of course, if you are contemplating suicide please visit the National Suicide Prevention Hotline immediately.

I have all of those numbers on my website.

Nikki Dubose Video Interview: **https://youtu.be/11Oc2bhyjEc**

Nikki's Website: **http://www.nikkidubose.com**

"Washed Away from Darkness to Light: A Memoir" by Nikki Dubose **http://amzn.to/2j2MRre**

Chapter 18

Michele Croswell

"I could never be truly happy unless I was putting myself first. And to put myself first, I needed to start speaking the truth."

~Katie Devine

At approximately two years old, my grandfather began to play with me and committed oral sex in my vagina. I don't recall him penetrating my vagina. He expired several years later.

Also my dad, the son of my grandfather began to fondle and penetrate me around the age of 3 after I began to gyrate on him as I sat in his lap (this is what my dad stated why he began to have sex with me).

He continued to have sex with me until the age of 13, after I stabbed him, threatened to tell and finally, became a run away. He taught me a lot on how to be promiscuous by teaching me that sex was love. He always told me I was his best lover and would buy me wonderful toys and as I got older around 10, he started giving me money.

(My dad always stated that if I told our secret it would destroy the family and he would have to hurt someone. Dad was known for being a physically abusive alcoholic. Back in the 60's we were considered a middle class family, with both of my parents working. But domestic violence was very prominent in our home.)

Where are you now in your healing journey?

I am happily & independently single by choice.

I am an overachiever and currently I am working at being a successful entrepreneur by writing my books and growing my travel business.

Because of all that I am involved with, including being a Care Coordinator for the elderly, as well as doing missionary trips out of the country. I have no time to focus on the negative history in my past.

I must admit I am a work in progress when it comes to any type of commitment involving a male counterpart that I might have interest in as well as he having an interest in me.

It has been decades since I have been in a committed relationship. I was a victim, now a survivor, who lives, loves, laughs, learns and grows with each second that I am blessed with.

I wrote a book about my abuse and that started my healing process.

After being violated, yes you may find it very difficult to trust anyone. I suggest reaching out to R.A.I.N.N 800-656-HOPE (4673) or to your local, abuse centers in your community.

Speak about what you are feeling and what you encountered. The more you release verbally the easier your guilt and your burdens will be released.

Please know that whatever abuse that you encountered IT WAS NOT YOUR FAULT EVER.

Release and decrease your stress by speaking out. Seek counseling if needed.

R.A.I.N.N. is an excellent resource for communicating and offering local services available.

Michelle's book: Don't Run Away Make a Way Queen
https://g.co/kgs/XusXd3

Michelle's Video Interview: **https://youtu.be/MqrF4iDOzss**

Chapter 19

Shannon O'Leary

"I do not believe I came from the school of hard knocks. Instead I believe I am from the school of the most fortunate. I have been incredibly lucky to survive my past and have gone on to live a productive and fulfilling life. Thank heavens for the kind and generous people who guided me, helped and showed me that life can be amazing when you surround yourself with loving and caring friends and family."

~ Shannon O'Leary

My abuser was my father and the abuse started from a very early age. I grew up under the shadow of horrific domestic violence, sexual and physical abuse, and serial murder.

My father lived with multiple personality disorder and the incidents he inflicted on me and others were exceedingly traumatic and I still live with the scars. I was also witness to some horrific crimes.

Where are you now on your healing journey?

I am in a much better place now. I have the support of a wonderful partner, my five children and of course my mother.

I am still nervous about telling my story and hyper-sensitive to others criticism. I also still get frightened and have nightmares but by writing the book I found my sleep patterns have improved.

I suffer from post traumatic stress but try to fill my life with music, writing and the creative arts. If I am helping others to move forward away from their personal trauma through my story, I am truly happy for them.

What has been the most positive thing you have done for yourself as since you began your healing journey?

I feel it has been acceptance of my past.

Being excruciatingly honest with myself and trying to work through my feelings. I will never forget the past, in fact, everyday it is the first thing I think about when I wake up and the last thing before I go to sleep.

This is because sad memories often cloud the quieter moments of my life.

However, by accepting what happened and vowing that I will move on towards a better and more nurturing future has made me stronger. By writing my memoir, The Blood on my Hands, it helped me face my feelings and the traumatic events I experienced.

What words of wisdom can you offer to those who have just begun their own journey of healing?

Be honest with yourself and realize that you were the victim.

But while saying this, move on.

Do not remain in a victim's fog...claw your way out and forge ahead. Be determined to make a beautiful future for yourself.

A friend once told me after hearing my story that I have a PhD from the school of hard knocks and experience. I said, "No! I have a PhD from the school of the most fortunate, because I am alive today. I survived!"

Always remember that you are a strong and resilient person because you have gone through hell.

Be proud that you have come through your past and know that you will still have moments of despair. Accept these moments, live them and then take a deep breath and move forward, because you never know what lies around the corner.

Life is filled with golden moments that outshine the bad.

What resources can you recommend to those just beginning on their journey of healing?

Talk to friends or family who understand you. Vocalizing can help you work through your emotions.

Contact local support groups, online resources and help lines if you need outside assistance.

If you are in a violent situation get away from the perpetrator immediately before it escalates to an even higher level.

There are people who will help you.

I am in Australia and we have support groups for depression, domestic violence and abuse victims.

Just remember you are not alone as there many people that have suffered abuse in their past.

No one case is the same and everyone has a different way of coping with their distress and grief.

Talking to others or writing things down can help you clarify what you feel and what you intrinsically need to move forward.

Also become involved and do something for others. By doing this you can see that others have suffered too and you are not alone.

Shannon O'Leary's Story: **http://amzn.to/2i9K4ft**

Shannon's Video Interview: **https://youtu.be/ysTiFuxQxbg**

Chapter 20

Karen Mason

"One reason people resist change is because the focus on what they have to give up, instead of what they have to gain."

~ author unknown

My first recollection was when I was just a wee one around four years old. Our family was stationed on a remote Canadian Air force base where it was common for the parents to trade off babysitting for each other. I remember it vividly. My parent's friend, a neighbor, was babysitting us.

This particular night, Mr. M exposed himself to me in the bathroom and I was taken aback. Later the same evening he suggested that we play doctor. I asked him what that meant. He said, "I am sick and you are a nurse and you have to make me feel better." It did not feel right and I told him I did not want to play that game.

Later, on another occasion, he exposed himself to me at the base grocery store. Later that night when my mom was bathing us kids, (in those days all of us kids were bathed together). I looked at my brother and said to my Mom, "Mr. M has one just like that only bigger."

My Mom was shocked and went immediately to Mr. M's wife and told her that he was to never be around her children again or she would turn him into the base commander.

Then when I was ten, my parents sent me and a sibling to stay with our uncle and his wife. My Uncle sat us down with a bunch of porn magazines and said he would be teaching us about biology. We were not allowed to wear underwear to bed. We were told it was "dirty". I know something happened during our sleep, but I do not remember exactly what . . . I only recall the feeling something did not feel right. On a sunny day, where we were only inside, he insisted on rubbing suntan lotion on my bare chest.

Even though the events with my uncle did not traumatize me, it certainly left an impact.

The worst and most crippling assault was when I was a young woman. I wore this trauma for over twenty years. I was working for a credit union in a private office where there was no public access. The admin staff was female and all managers were male.

I was not accepted in this environment. The women not only did not care for me, they bullied me on a regular basis. They were very mean; I was ostracized and teased about the way I walked. I was always excluded and left alone in the office during lunch breaks. Turns out, one of the managers picked up I was alone in the office during these times.

Because I did not have much money, I rode my bike to work and often it was very cold. When he could, he would give me a ride home in bad weather. I always thought that he was just being nice to me. He was the only one in the office who was kind to me.

That Christmas the company threw a holiday staff party. Naturally I hung out with Jim. Towards the end of the night, he asked if I wanted to share a cab ride home. As we drove home he asked if I wanted to grab a bite to eat. I was hungry and said yes. We pulled into an A&W (in those days you ordered from and ate in the car). Once we got our orders, he sexually assaulted me. I was screaming for him to stop. The cab driver did nothing. He just sat there like nothing was happening. I finally got Jim to stop, in time, and I was taken home. This assault floored me. The man had a pregnant wife at home. I thought he was my friend. I did not know what I had done to create this situation. I was friendly but I never considered, for a moment, I was ever flirting with him.

A short time later, alone again during a lunch break, he approached me. He shoved me into a corner and sexually assaulted me again. I did manage to get away from him and ran into the women's bathroom.

As I was in the bathroom, crying my heart out, one of the women came in when she back from lunch. I told her what happened. Her words were "You deserved it." The hardest part of this is that this woman felt I deserved it. The very next day I was fired. Jobs were scarce. I had no job. But because it was "my fault" I did nothing. I was full of shame, guilt and did not understand. This was about 30 years ago.

Following that assault, I experienced a couple of date rapes. I "earned those as well". To hold on to that guilt and shame for so long was incredibly painful. My self-esteem could not have been lower. My shame was crippling.

Where are you now on your healing journey?

Afterwards, in the mid '80's, I got into a physically, emotionally, sexually and extremely verbally abusive marriage. Five years in, I had a child with this man.

When he turned on our one year old child, I knew I had to break the chain of abuse so I left him. This is where my recovery began. I met with a counselor and she told me I was very strong for getting out of this relationship. For some reason I bought it . . . hook, line and sinker! I bought it I was strong. It was the first time in my life I actually believed I was strong. Up until this point, I thought I was one of the weakest pathetic human beings. I thought I was lower than pond scum. I had no self-confidence, unworthy of love, unworthy of anything good.

Needless to say, I have done a lot of self work which is still ongoing.

I took a course, the "Pursuit of Excellence" which in a nutshell is about accountability. It taught me so much about myself.

Today, I am confident. I feel good about myself. I feel good about how I look. I am remarried and love my husband. I have two wonderful sons. I am worthy of respect. I love my profession. I am worthy of deserving.

I have a thriving business and am so full of abundance. I truly have it all.

What words of wisdom would you share with someone deciding to make the changes so that they can heal?

I have been through my own personal hell and have lived to talk about it. If you are in an abusive relationship...get out! You do have a choice. When I left my first husband, I lost all of my [our] friends, I lost my home, I lost my standard of living, I lost the life I was living. To top it off, after I left him, he stalked me constantly. I had to move clear across the country to be safe.

I have survived and rebuilt. I took it on. You can too. I am not thankful that these things happened to me, but I am who I am because of where I have been.

I am proud of myself because I came from a background where there was no real encouragement to be strong. I surrounded myself with people who believed in me and helped build me up. Having women behind me who truly believed in me made all the difference.

If you are in an abusive situation don't believe the words the perpetrator says to you. Know who you are. Know you are good. Know you are beautiful. Find the right support. Surround yourself with people who believe in you who can kick you in the ass when you start feeling sorry for yourself, who won't buy your excuses and will listen to you when you need to talk.

Life does get better. Much better!

Sexual Assault Support Center: **https://www.facebook.com/ ColumbusSASC/?ref=br_rs&pnref=lhc**

Karen's Video Interview: **https://youtu.be/HA-u458VnOc**

Chapter 21

Renee Jean

"It is never too late to be who you were meant to be."

~Karen Sprecher

I am an author as well as a table games dealer. I live in Las Vegas. For me it was my first love as a teenager. He wasn't physically violent most of the time…it was the psychological abuse. He had me fully convinced that unless he said so, I was worthless and it took many years to get past that.

The starting point to begin my healing began many years later, through my first marriage and into my second. I struggled to do anything. I could not even walk across the street to get groceries, because what if I messed up, and forgot something, I did not want to let anybody down. I fought with that for a long time.

After my Dad passed away, I went back to school and finished getting my degree. As a celebration for graduating, I went to do volunteer work in Australia. There I had a very embarrassing situation. I fell off the trailer that we were being transported on. I slipped and got run over by the trailer and fell face down into a sheep pasture. I was mortified. I knew everyone would torment me and make fun of me. Instead they came over to help me. They showed me friendship. That is when I realized that it is ok not to be perfect. That everyone messes up. That I needed to get up, dust myself off and move on. That was without question the time when my healing began.

Later, when I embraced being a writer, and met other writers, began sharing our stories and that has been incredible for me. Being able to talk about my experiences helped me so much, as I have been able to understand that my problems are not unique, and I am not alone.

My healing came by working with my own personal support network. I opened up to my friends and family. Most of them did not know what I had gone through.

One friend of mine who is also a writer and I shared our stories with each other then decided to share our own stories with the world last October during Domestic Violence Awareness Month. We wanted to help others who are going through this same thing.

I also work with The Shade Tree organization here in the Las Vegas area.

I think the hardest thing as I started writing was that I had buried it for so long, that it brought everything forward.

My day job here at the Venetian, is so outstanding and supportive and opened up their ballroom for my book launch. I work with thousands of people and so many came to me and commented about how proud they are that I did this, good job and thank you.

It was incredible to have that kind of support. When I did the book launch, there was a police officer from the Las Vegas Metro police department who insisted that I needed to do a reading with my own voice.

One of the directors from The Shade Tree organization was there and came running over and hugged me. It was so helpful to be able to open up and share it with so many people. It was like nothing I have ever done. I am happy to be a friend to support someone going through difficult times.

What would you say to someone who was just starting down the road on their healing journey?

It is not going to be easy, but it is so totally worth it. There will be days that you want to run and hide. There will be days that you feel no one else will understand. But the important thing is that we do understand. We understand where you have been and what you are going through now. The feeling of wanting to run and hide and not talking about it… the feeling that no one else understands…that is why we have been quiet for so long.

You do not have to talk about it all of the time. I have not necessarily found an end to it yet. But, I honor myself on my off days. Some days I need the extra support and other days I am the one who gets to give it.

Renee's Book:

Survivor **http://amzn.to/2iJBSzm**

http://www.theshadetree.org/: Sheltering women, children and their pets

Renee's Video Interview: **https://youtu.be/YUKcU5W1Z4k**

Chapter 22

Tessa Milne

"Ignorance is not bliss, Ignorance is dangerous. Knowledge is bliss and powerful. Be bliss, be powerful!"

~ Tessa Milne

Tessa is an inspirational speaker survivor of abuse. She shares her survival story to inspire and motivate others to escape unhealthy and abusive lifestyles. Tessa also spreads awareness on ALL of the different forms of abuse to change and potentially save lives.

I was a child of abuse. My sister and I both were. My mother was the abuser and my father let it happen. We were conditioned to be submissive and not respond. It was our normal to deal with abuse and because I was used to it, I ended up in an abusive relationship in my early twenties that almost ended my life.

I was in that relationship for almost six years and it took me hitting rock bottom to understand that I needed to follow my happiness in order to stay alive. I was isolated and manipulated which are the two main tools that an abuser uses on their victims. I did not have any support or guidance and did not know there are resources available.

I attempted suicide and my failed attempt is what woke me up. It made me realize that I needed to do something to better myself. I found an outlet through animals. I started working with animals and that gave me the encouragement and unconditional love that I needed. I learned from animals that abuse is preventable and change is possible.

What advice would you share with someone just starting down the road of healing from abuse?

It was a process for me and it took several years. Many people expect the healing process to be fast and it is really not. The encouragement really starts with educating yourself and surrounding yourself with positive and like minded people.

For me, I did not have that. I had to learn this for myself the hard way and that is why it took me so long to heal.

Abuse comes in many different forms.

Abuse is preventable and change is possible with the proper support, guidance, inspiration and awareness. I now provide that for survivors.

The knowledge, which is the awareness, there is so much to learn, and it can be overwhelming. But when you surround yourself in positive environments, such as support groups and following your passion, counseling and therapy you find you do have rights and you do have a voice.

I joined support groups and I contacted attorneys to find out what my rights are. Reaching out for help is imperative.

It does not happen overnight. It takes tenacity.

How can we help stop abuse?

We educate ourselves on the issue! Learn all the different forms of abuse and spread awareness. Share your knowledge with someone you think might be going through abuse. Also, share with someone who isn't, because who knows, they might know someone who is!

Even an inspirational speaker needs inspiration. I get that from the survivors. The more that I am able to create the awareness and give guidance to those who are in this position, the better I feel.

When someone decides to make the change and they actually follow through with it, it is such an amazing feeling.

Tessa's Website: **http://faceofasurvivor.com**

Tessa's Video Interview: **https://youtu.be/EvSlBUbGMN0**

Chapter 23

Roberta Brown

"If you're broken, you fill yourself with broken people."

~Iyanla Vanzant

"If you don't ask, you don't get."

~Roberta Brown

My story starts as a little girl who was always terrified of everything. I had a rage-filled father and a complicit mother. It was never safe in my home. There were alcohol issues with my father.

There was always a battle of wills with my father. He was full of rage and hit me a lot. It was so difficult and I guess I did not realize that it was not that way in everyone's home.

The turning point for me was when I was sixteen, my father tried to kill me. He was so full of rage. He was bashing my head into the floor, I could feel myself passing out and I knew if I did not get away I would die.

I did get away with just the clothes on my back and no shoes. I do not remember where I found a phone and called my boyfriend.

My boyfriend found me wandering around, and took me back to his dorm room. He was in his first year of college and when he took me there, the resident advisor jumped into action because I was so swollen and beaten. They ran for ice and packed my back, head and shoulders. They said they would call the police and I begged them not to.

I ended up staying at the dorm and driving myself to school every day so that I could graduate from high school.

I did go home to get some clothes and my parents would not let anybody in the house to help me get my things, so I had to pack all my things by myself.

I have PTSD like so many survivors do.

I ended up moving in with that boyfriend. We were caretakers of an apartment building. He ended up being an abuser as well. I ended up staying with this guy for quite some time. At the time I asked myself, which was more humiliating, being beaten by my father or by my boyfriend.

When we grow up with the familiarity of abuse, we think we deserve it. I think over the years, I attracted abusive relationships. At least that's what felt "normal" for lack of a better term.

I was not settled for so many years…there was always so much drama in my life. I spent a lot a time trying to stay under the radar and not bring attention to myself. I was always trying to be a people pleaser. It never really mattered how hard I tried over the years, it was never consistent.

You wrote a book about your experience, what prompted you to write it and what did the writing of it do for you?

I decided I was not willing to keep the secrets of our family any longer. We were from a well respected and loved middle class Jewish family.

I was not willing to sit with the secrets any longer. I needed to figure out my life and the magnitude of PTSD and other issues I suffered with.

It took me about a year to write the book. I cried a lot as I wrote it. Before publishing I had a number of people read the book, and the response was what helped me so much.

They were grateful that my words helped them to put the puzzle pieces together for themselves in their own family situations.

What would you say to those who were just starting a journey of healing?

Breathe deeply. Look into yourself and know how good you are. Know that you did not choose this. Find a good therapist. Broach the subject with trustworthy people.

The most important thing is to love yourself and give yourself a break. Don't be so hard on yourself. Don't blame yourself. Be gentle with yourself and change the words you speak to yourself.

Don't minimize your experience and don't make excuses for the abuser.

There is healing from sharing your story.

Stand in your truth and be your authentic self.

Roberta's book:

"The Shoulding – A Story of Resiliency and Hope"
http://amzn.to/2iH6Qs1

Roberta's Interview: **https://youtu.be/nzLdx_SD3wo**

www.robertabrown.net

Chapter 24

Terri Lanahan

I'm 56 years old, have three children and five grandchildren and live in Butte, Montana. I am a survivor of childhood sexual abuse and adult domestic abuse.

I share my stories by means of poetry. I feel my poetry is a gift I was given. Poetry became my outlet. When you have been abused you feel so alone. When there was no one to tell, and no one to talk to about it, a big part of abuse is the isolation and the loneliness you feel.

My poetry has been a way for me to get my story out and has helped me to heal.

When I was 26 years old I was having severe flash backs, and anxiety over the abuse I had experienced. I ended up in a six week treatment program. Hearing words like "flash back," "anxiety attack," "panic attacks" I had never known there was a name for what I was experiencing. This put a name to my craziness. I thought I was going insane. This was when I was able to start expressing what happened to me and how I felt.

That is when I started channeling my story through my poetry. I had become so isolated, alone, depressed and desperate. Thank God for treatment programs because they really helped me walk through a lot of my pain.

What other tools did you tap into that helped you heal?

I am a volunteer advocate at our local shelter. I've been with them for over twenty years. This has been another channel for me. Working with these women and children, seeing their pain and their strength has given me courage. Many have walked away from everything and everyone sometimes. Their strength and courage has been amazing to witness.

What words of wisdom would you share with someone deciding that they want to start their healing journey?

It is painful, very painful when you start walking through the memories of the abuse. But is so worth it. The healing process is a beautiful process. I have an amazing life now. I could not have imagined the life I have now. I feel blessed. It all came from my recovery. Recovery was difficult, it was a struggle.

Not only did I have anxiety and depression, but I had turned to drugs and alcohol to numb myself from the pain, to sedate and medicate.

I had to stop both drugs and alcohol, but what a blessed and remarkable life I have now.

I would not be here without the strength of other women. It has opened doors for me and put me on a path of recovery.

Poem written by: Terri Lanahan

A fragile doll that stands on a shelf.
She bears the pain all by herself.
A doll you see but never hear.
She stands alone overwhelmed with fear.
As time passes by she fills the shelves with clutter.
If she felt alone her stomach would twist and flutter.
She didn't want to listen to the sounds of her own mind.
When her feelings and her thoughts would slowly unwind.
See... he always tried to shatter her when she was by herself.
Then he would place her back on the shelf.
So there she stands alone in her pretty dress.
No one sees that underneath she's a shattered and broken mess.
They do not see the tears on her porcelain face.
They do not see the blood that has stained her lace.
As time passes by she finds her pain only increases.
She realizes she has to mend all those broken pieces.

Terri's Video Interview: **https://youtu.be/lQYnBAVFsq8**

Chapter 25

Sylvia Goalen

"Peace is not the absence of conflict, but the ability to cope with it."

~Robert Fulghum

I don't talk about my story much. I guess it's easier to suppress the feeling or forget what happened years ago.

I remember being a child in Guatemala, my birth country. My parents were working on getting our family migrated to the U.S. My father left several months before us. We lived a large home with multiple generations living together. I remember playing as a child with all of my cousins. No one knew it was the perfect environment for abuse to happen.

I don't remember my exact age, but I was in 1st or 2nd grade when the abuse began. I currently have a daughter in 2nd grade, and when I look at her it brings tears to my eyes.

How could someone take advantage of such a young child? To this day I have a hard time understanding and sympathizing.

I had an older cousin. He was about 16 or 17 at the time, who was very fond of me. He would often buy me candy, snacks and let me be the lead when we played games with the rest of the kids. Little did I know that this was how the abuse would begin; he was grooming me.

It started with a hug, and that lead into him trying to touch me inappropriately. I was uncomfortable and scared, but fearful of how angry he would get if I was to tell. I remember the small incidents, but the one that scares me the most was the first time he pinned me down on my mother's bed and took advantage of me. I've never felt pain like that before. It's hard to describe and I immediately felt numb. When he was done, he threatened me. He threatened that if I told, my father would never come back for us. I was terrified. The abuse continued until we moved to the United States.

By the time I was a teen, I wasn't the best daughter or role model for any of my siblings. I never listened to my parents and did what I wanted, with no regard for people's feelings. I snuck out multiple times, hung out with the wrong crowd, lost my virginity at a young age, and never truly understood how I should treat my body. I felt numb most of the time. I started drinking, experimented with drugs, and did a lot of things that I am not very proud of.

At about 16 years of age, my parents announced that a relative would be coming to live with us from Guatemala. When they announced his name, I felt as if the world was crushing down on me and everything I knew. The cousin who took everything from me as a child would be moving in with us. He moved in and it was as if nothing had happened. I avoided him as much as I could.

About a year after he moved in, my parents announced they were going out of the country for a few weeks and my cousin would be in charge. I really didn't put too much thought into it since I really didn't care much about anything. In the meantime, I had started dating a boy who truly loved me and understood me. We were making plans for a future together. The day before my parents came back into town, I invited several friends over, including my boyfriend. My cousin caught us making out, kicked my boyfriend and friends out, and came back into my room to yell at me. I remember him telling me in Spanish how "good" he was going to make me feel, like he used to back in Guatemala. But this time I was almost 17. I was grown and was able to fight off my attacker. I ran away from home and refused to come home until my parents returned.

When my parents came home I was ready to tell them everything. I told them what happened, only for my mother to call me a liar. She made me confront my attacker. He called me a spoiled teen who was making up stories so I wouldn't get in trouble. My father looked at my tears and knew it was real. It took everything in him to keep from hurting my cousin. After all of this, it was never mentioned again.

Shortly after that incident, I found out I was four months pregnant with my first son. He was born premature just two and a half months later. He has been the best thing that has ever happened to me. My first love, the first man that I knew would never leave or betray me.

Fast forward to when I was 29 years old, married with one son and working on adopting our 2nd. Part of the adoption process was taking some parenting classes. The Latin American Association was hosting a *Stewards of Children*® training.

As I sat through the class it took everything inside me not to break down and cry when I learned about other survivors. After the training I went up to the facilitator and thanked her. I told her I was a survivor.

I didn't deal with my abuse until I became an adult. It took me many years to come to terms with what had been done to me and to build strong and trusting relationships with the people who loved me.

I want everyone to know that child sexual abuse is not ok and that our job as adults is make sure our children and communities are safe. I will continue to advocate for the children that do not have a voice of their own.

I ask you to join me in supporting prevention training. Your donation with train adults across the country, and those adults will be better equipped to protect the children in their lives.

I know we can live in a world that allows children to grow up happy, healthy and safe.

Please visit **http://bit.ly/d2lpossible** to see our vision for ending child sexual abuse.

Or make a donation here: **http://bit.ly/d2ldonate**

Chapter 26

Souraya Christine

"Unforgiveness is like drinking poison and expecting the other person to die."

~ Pastor Clinton House

As a survivor of child sexual abuse, I'm writing to you with a story of hope. Although I experienced the trauma of abuse as a child, I have seen the power to protect children when adults are trained in child sexual abuse prevention.

My abuse first started when I was five years old by a cousin who often visited. I was afraid of her and so I would do what she told me to do.

Then at 7 years old, my mother's live-in boyfriend started sneaking into my room at night. For many years, my mom didn't realize what was occurring and would leave me alone with him a lot. I had a sister who was younger than me and I was afraid for her. I never wanted him to touch her so I always stayed. I had people that cared about me that I could go to, but was afraid if I left he would turn on her.

I thought it was a dream. I didn't believe it was happening.

I was 11 years old when it finally came to an end. One day my mom and grandmother came home from shopping and found me crying. I had just had enough. My grandmother sensed something wasn't right and her first question to me was, "Did he touch you?" I said, "Yes." I told them it had been going on for years.

My mother put him out and we went to court. He ended up with 18 months in prison. It left me with a lot of anger and a lot of pain. We never spoke of it in my family and I never received counseling.

You don't think about how abuse can impact you and who you become. You attract negativity and bad situations into your life because you never dealt with the pain. You don't realize the affects that it has. And so I dealt with it the best I knew how.

I held a lot of resentment towards my mom for a lot of years. I didn't understand how she didn't know. I have since forgiven her, but I do still wonder sometimes how it happened. How so you leave your child with a person who is hurting them?

I know my mom didn't plan to let someone hurt me; she just didn't have the skills to protect me from my abusers and to deal with me telling.

It molded a lot of my decisions and a lot of my behaviors into adulthood. For me, it was a matter of trust. I had other issues as a result of rape and date rape, and those things compounded the pain I had from my childhood abuse. It brought me to the point where I didn't trust people. I became cold, angry, and bitter at the world. It was more awful for me than the people that dealt with me.

Thankfully, through faith and personal development I was able to heal and experience tremendous joy in my life.

After leaving an emotionless marriage, I decided to focus on myself. I realized I had issues that I needed to deal with and turned my attention to self-development. After reading some self-help books, I realized I had been unhappy my whole life. I didn't remember any states of happy at all. I was in my 30's and had never been happy.

That realization hit me very hard and I decided I needed to learn how to be happy. I tried marriage, and parenthood, but I needed to change something deep inside of me to really be happy. I set out to find happiness. I wanted to be able to smile and feel what my face was showing.

I was on my way to church and when I walked through the doors I literally felt weight lifted off of me. I wasn't expecting it, I wasn't even totally ready for it, but I didn't stop crying from the time I walked in to the time I got in my car. This happened weekly. I felt like the pastor was speaking directly to me and some issue I was trying to deal with. This is what I was looking for.

Finding God was a new beginning and that's what gave me the happy. The spiritual aspect is what helped to heal me.

I realized that I hadn't gone through any healing process. The pastor one Sunday started talking about forgiveness and he said, "Not forgiving is like drinking poison and expecting the other person to die." It hit me like a ton of bricks. This is what I had been doing my whole life. The problem was me, and I was the one that needed to do the healing. That started the process and I started in that moment to let go of things and come to terms with what had happened to me.

I was strong enough to endure because I am standing here today and someone else needs to know that they can survive, too. Someone else needs to hear that you are beautiful and you deserve to be here. I find joy in helping other people and being of service.

I can't undo my past, but I am strengthened by the help I can provide other people. I also know that children in the future can be better protected from sexual abuse when the adults in their lives take prevention training.

Please visit **http://bit.ly/d2lpossible** to see our vision for ending child sexual abuse.

Or make a donation here: **http://bit.ly/d2ldonate**

Chapter 27

Christina Wensell

"Scars remind us where we have been, they don't define where we are going."

~ David Rossi

I will start by saying I was a happy child and very outgoing, I was a child that was known by everyone on the block, and I was not afraid of anything. I loved life. My parent's joke would be that I wouldn't ever need drugs because life was my drug.

I am not exactly sure the day or year that abuse entered my life, but my memories start at about the age of 11 or 12. I suffered several years of not only sexual abuse but mental manipulation. I feared telling my mother or others because of threats from my abuser, who was my father.

My father prior to this was my idol. I wanted to do and be everything he was. Many memories I have a hard time recalling. I don't remember friends, birthdays, and pieces of my life. They come to me in sections. The abuse went on for about 4 to 5 years. The last time will always be very vivid in my mind. My mother walked in on my father sexually abusing me. I remember my mother hitting my father and asking him what he was doing. All I wanted to do was become invisible, to run and never come back. He always said that my mom would kick me out of the house and stand behind him if I ever told, and that was what I believed would happen.

From that day on my life changed. My mother made me move my room from downstairs, where I was independent to upstairs where she could watch me. I had new rules that I could not wear bedroom PJs around the house, and had to be fully clothed before leaving my room. It felt as if it was my fault.

I was the one with new rules and being punished. I was briefly talked to about the abuse and then it was a closed subject. I was not to tell anyone, because my father was well known and it would hurt his reputation and his business. I felt ashamed.

Blanking of the memory is very common and often is for our protection. Where are you now in your healing process Christina?

I would say that a lot of times I am the top of my game. I can be doing well, and then all the sudden something will crash me down and I am that little girl again trying to make sense of what is happening to me.

I still have flashbacks at times, but I try to have an action plan in mind when they happen. I really enjoy our "Woman I Love" group on Facebook for that. I enjoy being able to talk to others that have gone through similar situations and learn how they have been able to overcome what they have gone through.

I am a mother of 2 beautiful daughters. During the process of them growing up I stumbled, but I also learned about myself. I have been joyful for them during their proms, and boyfriends and teen years, but then also sad for the little girl that I was and never grew up to experience.

I went through those adventures with prom and such, friends saw me but it was a mask. I wore many masks during my years. I am now taking down those masks and trying to find the me that is underneath them.

I have been married for 28 years. We have had a lot of struggles and many of them have had to do with the abuse I suffered. I also married a man who in some ways was a lot like my dad.

My husband abused drugs and alcohol for many years. I had to become the backbone of our home rather than my husband. I think due to my past I never let my husband really bond with our children. I never wanted him to get that close. In the back of my mind I felt that he would end up hurting them to. I really put a wall up with them and him, and then on the other hand let them have a grandparent relationship with their grandfather.

In many ways, I think this goes back to the mental manipulation after the abuse. I was told the abuse was because my father was an alcoholic, or because my mother was not there for him. It was excused because she was not doing her wifely duties, since her father passed away.

I continued this thinking for years. The alcohol was to blame, so to me that was the threat not my father. I guess in many ways it helped me with my day to day with my relationship with my kids and family in a whole.

Christina, I have watched you make some remarkable changes in this past year. What do you attribute your changes to?

I had started writing my book to tell my story several years ago, and then set it aside. I have now picked it up again and continued my writing. My book has been my soul kind of searching out who I am. Writing down what happened to me and taking the masks off one by one and trying to find that what they call the "Inner child". I needed to find her. I needed to get those feeling out that have been buried deep inside, and let them loose.

I also have been able to talk to my daughters. I let them read portions of my book to try to help them to better understand why I did the things I did when they were young. Why I would run out of my parents' house screaming and dragging them out by their hair, because I was so emotionally upset I needed to get out of there.

They found out a little of what happened to me, but never knew how it affected me. I could not express those feelings to them as children; they were too young to understand. I did not want to affect their relationship with their grandparents and their view of them or scare my girls. I did not feel that I had that right.

In my book I put my feelings out there. I don't hold back. You can see me in every sentence you read, and I don't think I ever have expressed those feelings or words to anyone. It really is a work of love. Love for others, and love for my family. Love for myself for the strength I had to get through. I wouldn't have ever known what I went through without it.

I read chapters back to myself, and I am proud of myself for surviving.

I am learning every day, but I am growing. My journey has not ended and I am looking forward to the next chapters.

Did you tap into any resources, like books that you have read or courses that you have looked at, that have helped you?

I am an avid reader, I love to read. I can't pinpoint really any book that I would say helped me more than another one. I do like books that make me use many of my own resources though. I enjoy not only reading but interacting in the book.

One book that did do that was: "The Courage to Heal Workbook, by Ellen Bass and Laura Davis. I would say this book was the one that started me on my road to recovery.

Music also helps me heal, and I have used many lyrics in my own personal book.

If someone else was starting down this road of healing, what would you say to them?

I guess the first thing is to know it is not and was not your fault. Then the next is that, you are not alone. Seek out someone you can talk to that you can basically unload your feelings without feeling resentment, or feeling ashamed. I really needed that when I was going through this process.

When I reported what happened to me the resolution was to take pills. Pills were not the answer I was looking for. It only got me further and further into depression. Sometimes you need just a listening ear, not even someone to say something, just to be able to unload.

I also would suggest that you write down your feelings. You don't have to write a book, but sometimes just writing it down and releasing it to the universe and out of our bodies heals. I started out just writing in a diary, and I would even jot down my mood and the time of the day I was writing. Looking back on it days or months later, I was able to tell what some of my triggers were and what to avoid or what I needed to work through just because of my notes.

Give yourself encouragement. Write on your mirror that you are beautiful, just to remind yourself that every day. This was and still is hard for me. I think all of us have very bad self-image problems that go through this. I use to weigh almost 500 pounds and I know that my weight was my security blanket, much like a coat I wore when I was in High School.

Find yourself a support team, like I have found in The Woman I love.

We don't have to be just survivors, we can thrive. We can be happy. That is what this whole book project is about, and what our whole message is. We can't change what happened to you, but we can change what happens next.

Exactly, and that is another thing. We need to recognize what we did go through. When I have read parts of my story and reflect on different parts of it I step back and say, Wow. I can't believe I survived that. I am still here.

You are here with us today. Look at what beautiful qualities you have that resulted from the fact that you made that choice! It took courage and determination.

That is so true. My daughters all the time tell me how strong they think I am. We have become so close now because I am able to explain so much to them that when they were little they only saw how upset their mommy would be at times and not quite sure of why. They were able to have a relationship with their grandfather whom they really loved and felt highly of him.

I never wanted my image of my childhood to reflect on their relationships. I did protect them, but kept my impact and feelings away from it. I did not share those feelings. I felt others would use my words for their own motives.

This is the first time I am sharing any of this publicly. Many people who know me are going to be shocked. It is hard to step out of that box and say I am a survivor, and this happened to me. I no longer want to give strength to the abuse. It no longer has power over me. I want to help others in doing this.

You most certainly will Christina, and as you daily learn to stand on your story and not in it, you will discover strengths you never knew you had. You are here for a purpose. Know that you are in the right place at the right time, and that we are locking arms and hearts so that together we can be a part of the change so needed in our world.

I believe that with my whole heart.

Christina's Video Interview: **https://youtu.be/DIMmgLbfJL4**

Chapter 28

Teresa Syms

"There is nothing more beautiful and powerful than the courage of a woman."

~ Teresa Syms

At almost fifty-seven years old, I reflect back on my life and think, "Who is that person that survived all of those horrors?" "Why is she still here and how did she endure the beatings, the sexual abuse from her father and family physician and psychological trauma from her sister, mother, and ex-husband."

Allow me to give you some background.

I was born to first generation Canadians whose parents emigrated from Belgium in the early 1900's. My father's side of the family has been plagued for four generations over lies and secrets of incest, physical violence, alcoholism and suicide.

My mother's family, were hard working people, who also had emigrated from Belgium in the early 1900's. However, my mother, as a young woman, started losing her hearing, and went completely deaf shortly thereafter, which compounded her psychological and emotional problems. She suffered from depression, anxiety, panic attacks and agoraphobia. Her early life with my father had been extremely difficult.

They worked hard and endless hours on my father's parent's tobacco farm in the 1950's. My mother lost her first three pregnancies as stillbirths. When she finally had my sister in 1957, she was beside herself with joy. She had a child, a girl, nothing else mattered and above all, she did not want any more children.

Three years later, my parents went bankrupt, from a severe loss on the sale of the year's tobacco crop. They lost their home, income, and the friction within the family hit critical points.

Then, never expecting to have any more children my mother soon discovered she was pregnant. She was furious! My father, happy to have another child had to contain his joy in order to not upset the delicate balance of his wife's sanity. She hated him for the pregnancy.

In June 1960, I was born and my parents were horrified. I was born crippled. "Clubfeet," the doctor called it. Both of my legs were twisted from the hips, with my toes turning inward to face behind me. My mother didn't want me before I was born, and now she was angry at what she was stuck with and the extra work caring for me would entail.

At seventeen days old, the doctor applied my first set of casts, from toes to hips, complete with a steel bar between my ankles to space my legs apart and keep them straight.

Once I was brought home, my sister took an instant dislike towards me as she now had to share her parents with this other kid. Until I came along, she was an only child, and a spoiled one at that. She didn't take kindly to having to share. The extra attention I received created a hatred within her that remains to this day.

Luckily after two years of casts and wearing the steel brace, my legs were straight and grew strong and very active child.

Because we were left alone at a very young age, my sister decided I was her punching bag. The indignities and trauma I suffered at her hands was enough for any lifetime. One day, around the age of four years old, I was sick with the flu. I wanted some ginger ale but she refused to get a glass down for me, so I drank from the bottle. I knew I was not to drink from the bottle but I desperately needed a drink. As I lifted the bottle to my mouth to take a drink, my sister slapped her hand on the end of the bottle, causing the bottoms of my two front top teeth to chip. I knew I was going to be in big trouble when the parents found out. There was no way I wanted to tell them, so she decided to take the upper hand and tell on me. If I was blamed for doing something, they always ignored what she had done.

When they arrived home much later, my sister told her tale first, claiming she was trying to take the pop bottle away from me and I fought back, causing my teeth to chip. Always believing her word against mine, I received the leather belt across my behind several times. That night, still sick with the flu, and yet hungry because I was denied dinner, I lay in bed later crying into my pillow wondering what I had done wrong. Unfortunately, I had to share a bed with my tormentor, and she just lay there laughing at me.

This was the mildest of what I endured as a young child. At the age of five, we moved houses and the bedroom I was assigned was nice, and I didn't have to share it with anyone. But the closet was painted dark blue and it scared me terribly. It looked like a black hole. My sister saw my fear and on moving day when my parents were not around, she pushed me into the closet and then blocked the door. Kicking, screaming and crying I begged to be let out. She laughed. As my anger and rage built, I was able to push open the door. She ran into the kitchen and I followed. When I caught up to her, she once again laughed in my face. I gave her one punch directly in the stomach and she hit the floor, completely winded. Tears bubbled up in her eyes and so did her hate of me.

I knew now I was in serious trouble. Running back to my new bedroom I hid under the bed. Thinking this was not a very safe place to hide, I stepped into the most terrifying place on earth...my closet. "If I hide just right they won't find me," I thought. Time passed and for some reason the house was silent.

Suddenly I heard my father's booming voice bellowing my name. My closet door flew open. A large rough hand reached inside, grabbed me by the arm and pulled me from my hiding place. I knew I was in serious trouble. As usual, my father had been drinking heavily that day.

Most of the men that were helping with the move were his drinking buddies. He reeked from beer.

At first, I was emotionally, verbally and psychologically battered by him, all the while my sister and mother stood watching the punishment, with smiles on their faces. Next I was ordered to pull up my pant legs and was forced to kneel on a very special board of my father's own design. He had saved his beer caps from his drunken state the previous night and had nailed the caps to a piece of plywood. The caps were perfectly place in a grid pattern, pointed side up. I was ordered to kneel on this torture device until he said I could move. If my posture was slouched, I received the leather belt across my bottom. If I cried out, the belt came for that as well. As tears rimmed my eyes, I looked up. It was then I realized I was looking into a mirror at an unwanted, hated, five year old girl. Over the next few years, I assumed this position many times, all the while looking into the mirror and hating the girl that looked back at me.

Not only was I rejected by my family, but also later from my first boyfriend.

We actually had fallen madly in love, much to his mother's dislike. I was alright to date, but she didn't want him to get serious about me because, "she comes from a bad home." Even though he didn't care about family history, our relationship was a rocky one. He was the first person I loved and who loved me, but every now and then, he wanted his freedom and left me. I grew depressed and my mother's answer was to take me to see the family doctor for my depression and to be put on birth-control pills.

The doctor had his own special way of examining me. Every time I went in for a pill refill, he would perform an internal exam, probing my insides and asking me each time to let him know if I became over-stimulated by his hands. I had no idea this was wrong. I was only fourteen years old. Who could I ask? Certainly not my mother! After all, she is the one that took me to him. I wanted the pills, so, thinking this was 'normal,' I submitted.

The doctor's solution for my depression was tranquillizers. My mother agreed. At first they helped calm me, but the drugs did nothing to help me recover from the abuse, loneliness and fear I lived in constantly.

Like the rest of my family, I soon began to drink heavily. I started drinking at fourteen years old and at seventeen, decided my life wasn't worth living anymore. One cold, winter night, I was already feeling the effects of the several glasses of whiskey I had consumed. However, the agony I felt was still there. Then I remembered the pills. After taking two of the tranquillizers, I announced I was going out for a drive. No one cared if I left, or that I had too much to drink. My path was set and I knew the exact spot where I would end my suffering. As I drove, tears poured down my face. There was nothing good in this life for me. So I knew I had to end this existence. In the distance I spotted the massive maple tree I fully intended to drive the car into. The night was dark and out in the country, no one would see what I was going to do. Aiming for the tree, I said my last prayer and drove towards my end.

About fifty feet before the impact, I felt the steering wheel being pulled from my hands. Someone was turning the car back onto the road. It's not possible! I was alone in the car! But now, hyper aware of my surroundings, I knew I was not in control of the steering wheel. "You are not finished here yet," I heard someone whisper into my head.

Now sobered by shock, I heard the words again, "You are not finished here yet." I stopped the car in the middle of the road and turned on the interior lights. Believing someone was playing a terribly cruel joke on me, I searched inside the vehicle, but I was alone! It was at this point that I realized my life was protected and I realized I had just met my guardian angel. He had extremely strong hands and a gentle voice that spoke so soothingly to me.

Obviously, my life did not end that night. Eventually I married a young man who I thought would take care of me. I was wrong! After helping him pay for his divorce, his first marriage had failed after eighteen months, I realized I was in too deep, but it was better than being at home with my parents.

We married in September of 1981. In all of our wedding pictures my new husband's right hand was hidden. He had a cast on it. Ten days prior to our wedding date, we were at a harvest party, where he had too much to drink and being tired from working a great deal, he passed out. With the help of a few young men, I got him into the car and headed for home.

At this time in my life, I was strong-minded, argumentative and didn't know when to keep quiet some times. Unfortunately, this was one of those times. As I drove and complained about his behavior, he decided to back-hand me across the face to shut me up. Hearing a loud crack inside my head, pain shot through my face and I was temporarily blinded. I slammed on the breaks and grabbed my face. I was in so much pain I was unable to speak. Once I regained my sight, I continued to drive home, in silence out of fear. When we arrived, I walked into the house, leaving him in the car. A few minutes later he staggered into the house and stood behind me in the kitchen while I had a drink of water. Suddenly the argument continued. When I saw his fist coming at my face, I had enough sense to move. His fist smashed into the three-quarter inch plywood cupboard door. Now he was in pain and backed away. I had a terrible headache so I went into the bedroom, locking the door behind me.

Hours later, I heard a gentle tapping on the door. He begged me to come out and drive him to the hospital. He believed he had broken his hand when he punched the door.

As he was being x-rayed for the break, the doctor questioned me as to how it happened. I told the truth and laughed slightly as I thought he deserved the pain of a broken hand. What I didn't realize was the doctor was looking for signs of abuse in me. Even though I had been hit straight across the face, there was no damage visible; no black eyes, swelling or bleeding.

During our many years together, I experienced two more breaks to my nose, verbal and emotional turmoil and three miscarriages and countless reconstructive surgeries/joint fusions on my left foot. Because I had been quite an athlete when I was young, my left ankle was wearing down, hence the need to fuse the joints. However, my two greatest gifts in my life were my sons, who are now strong, large grown men.

When looking back, I realized I had lived a very abusive and unhappy life, believing that I had made this mistake and must make the best of it. During twenty-five year marriage, no matter how hard I tried, I was never good enough, didn't speak correctly, didn't behave properly and always received the instructions before we went somewhere as to how I should behave and humiliated when I spoke, so eventually I stopped speaking in my own home.

For the first several years of our marriage, I faced migraine headaches daily. Rarely did a day go by, where I didn't have a headache of at least a seven on a scale of zero to ten. While working full time at a school, with two small children, living in perfectionist syndrome, and having my less than sane mother baby-sit my children while I worked. I would have such extreme migraines that I would drive myself to the hospital or doctor's office for a shot of Morphine or Demerol to help take away the explosions in my head. After receiving the shot, I would pick up my children and go home. My boys were very well behaved and played quietly in the same room with me while I slept.

A person can only take so much of this before your life hits a critical state. I felt alone, unloved, unwanted and miserable. Many times I would ask, beg and plead with my husband to get help to fix our marriage. As per usual, it was my fault, because he claimed I was crazy or depressed.

In my forties, I became the live-in caregiver to my paternal grandmother. A woman who showed she loved me by helping me financially throughout the years. Now it was my turn to give back. She lived with us for almost ten years. Feeling she was too much of a burden on me, she went into a nursing home. It was here, just before she died that I told her I was divorcing my husband. Her words to me were, "I told you not to marry him." I was relieved she understood, and I laid my head in her lap and cried. A few weeks later, my grandmother died at the age of ninety-one.

Now at forty-three years old, I was faced with several major changes I needed to make in order to survive. My grandmother's death rocked me to the core. She was my hero and a woman who was more mother to me than my own, and other than my sons, the last family member I had. Soon, I had lost track of who I was, my purpose, and the direction I was going.

Now faced with living on my own for the first time in my life, I was terrified and excited even though this was something I had prayed for, for many years. My first independent choice was to attend college for Business Administration. After living alone for almost two years, I moved from Brantford to London to be with my fiancé, a man who encouraged me and supported me in everything I tried. Together we escaped the traumas of our previous marriages and began to live our dreams.

In 2005, I changed direction slightly. I transferred to Fanshawe College in London for a diploma in Business, majoring in Human Resources. My life was falling into place perfectly, or so I thought.

Combining two years in one, the gauntlet was dropped. I had a new home complete with two challenging step-sons, and my two grown sons, who lived in a house my grandmother helped finance, along with a narcissistic ex-wife who refused to accept reality. However, school remained my main focus, until a teacher's strike brought my education to a standstill. Not being one to take things lying down, I challenged the system. In the meantime, I had received an offer of employment from a local manufacturer of armored vehicles. The choice was difficult. I wanted my education but I could not pass up the job offer. So, I made a deal with the school principal. The principal agreed to give me my education because the course would be completed in two months, and there didn't seem to be a quick end to the strike. With that agreed to, I took on the job.

My new career in Training and Development was good as long as you understood the hierarchy within the department. There were those directly above me who had no background in Human Resources, but because they were grandfathered in from another company, they had the control.

Suddenly the teachers strike ended and the principal reneged on their deal with me. If I didn't return to school full time, I would lose my diploma. Now in fighting mode, I pushed back and a compromise was reached. I kept my job and attended one class per week. My employer agreed, and I graduated with honors.

In June of 2006, I celebrated my marriage to Don. My life had turned around and I was happy for the first time. Yes, we had children and ex-spouse issues, but together we could conquer anything. Or so we thought.

Leaving work in February 2007, I was faced with a horrific winter storm. I was confident in my driving skills and my Dodge Ram. The roads were slick with ice and the strong north wind made driving conditions treacherous. I took my time and was careful. Suddenly, I noticed an oncoming truck that was losing control. The vehicle was spinning, sliding and veering across the road. Wanting to give the oncoming truck room, I stopped in my lane, as did the others around me. There was no escaping fate.

Braced with a death-grip on the steering wheel, my right foot pushed hard onto the brake pedal, and all senses on high-alert, I watched the truck shear off the side mirror from the vehicle in front of me. After several spins across the road, the truck now aimed directly at me. I was trapped inside my vehicle and in my own terror. Would I live? If I did, how badly injured would I be? Suddenly I saw my husband's face. Would I ever see him again? Terrified and braced for impact my body was hyper-vigilant. I will never forget the sights or sounds as long as I live. I believed I was going to die as I watched the truck hit me head-on. Fear and pain is what I felt and disaster is what I saw, but what I heard was, "You are not finished here yet." After the horrible impact, I waited for what seemed an eternity, for the emergency vehicles to arrive and remove me from my prison.

I was unable to move, unlike the women who hit me. With no feeling in my legs, pain in my neck and back, a witness approached me and said, "I smell gas!" He walked away to find the source and terror struck again as I thought my truck would explode with me trapped inside. When the witness returned he said it was not fuel, but fluid from my radiator.

Once transported to the local hospital, I spent the next five hours taped to a board. Hours later, I was released with a neck so fragile I could not support my own head. I had suffered severe soft tissue injuries from head to foot, a Type II Whiplash (third time), and ten fractured teeth. I lost my job, my income and all hope for my future. What I was not aware of yet, was the brain injury and Post Traumatic Stress Disorder that would affect me for the rest of my life.

For five years, I endured innumerable treatments, medical examinations, surveillance, lawyers and countless indignities by the insurance company. I was a victim of circumstance but pre-existing conditions led the insurance company to treat me as guilty, rather than innocent, which lowered my 'life' value in dollars and cents. I was mortified having my life laid on the table, and discussed as if I didn't exist. My entire life I had been a fighter, but suddenly, I lost the strength to fight. It took five years to settle my claim. Finally, I was free, but the accident left me with a brain injury, chronic pain and multiple injuries that would never heal.

For nine years I devalued and hated myself. Always asking, "What am I supposed to do with my life? Why was I not killed?" The settlement covered the huge debt incurred, but left me with very little.

I began writing a book based on secrets surrounding my family. Then I was asked to coordinate two internet radio programs. The work was liberating and allowed me the freedom to set my own schedule. Perfect! I became an entrepreneur. I had already tried and failed at working for someone else.

I took courses on authorship, leadership and personal growth. Then it was suggested that I become a coach. Here was a solid idea which meshed with my goals. My book, *A Century of Secrets*, was happening and my second goal of helping others was about to unfold as well.

My life mountain was massive but I have overcome all the obstacles. I was born crippled, survived a severely abusive childhood, an attempted suicide as a teenager, and an unhealthy, abusive marriage. The near-death experience that day in February made me see, ***"I'm not finished here yet"***.

Now almost ten years later, I am an entrepreneur, author, leader, personal and life empowerment coach. When I realized it wasn't my body that would make the difference, I changed. It is my heart, mind and strong will. I refuse to hide my gifts or not to show who I truly am. I have found my life purpose. I am a strong, powerful, and intuitive woman who will leave this world a better place if I help one person to see their own value and power.

Leaving adversity, a near death experience and childhood violence behind me, I gladly walk into the gifts of strength, courage and power. I have emerged as a powerful woman and welcome my future. This is why I launched Sterling Silver Coaching.

There is nothing more beautiful and powerful than the courage of a woman.

Teresa Syms, is the Author of: *A Century of Secrets*

Teresa Syms host of, Powering Through Life radio show:
www.encouragingyouradio.com

Website: **http://www.symssolutions.com**

Chapter 29

Sondra Joyce

I had been single for many years. I loved my life. I owned a spa in Northern Colorado in the late 80's and early 90's, before massage and spa treatments and holistic health were popular. My clinic was on the leading edge of health and healing. One of our regular clients said we should apply for nonprofit status, and call ourselves the Sisters of the Healing Hands.

As a group of amazing women, we truly transformed people's lives in our treatments, classes and retreats. This was before cell phones and the internet, and we had a huge circle of clients and friends that loved us and whom we loved deeply. We were not in "business" in the normal sense. We were spiritual beings committed to transformation. It was my personal delight to see women move from a contracted life to an expansive, loving experience. I felt deeply transformed doing this work as well. I walked in the world with so much love and compassion in my heart. Often I felt I was not really on this planet, but here as a facilitator to another world where divinity was the norm. I loved the book "The Kin of Ata is Waiting for You." I could relate to Jeff Bridges in the movie Fearless. I knew in my core that Atlantis and Lemuria were alive, past remembrances of ancient civilizations where unconditional love was the language. Martin Buber had a profound impact on me with his I/Thou philosophy. I chose not be separate from anything or anyone.

In my years from 27-42, I led what I would call a charmed life. I traveled extensively. I was an international speaker for the Whole Health Institute. I was part of a transformative spiritual community that touched me to the core of my being. I knew that I was a divine being, living a human life. During this time, I had 42 marriage proposals. Men would flock to me for my charisma, sensuality, and because I truly was "untouchable." I certainly had boyfriends, but never felt like I could cross over and devote myself wholeheartedly when I felt I was "married" to God, to my concept of the divine.

I could not understand depression or boredom. I was so happy and lively. I would think to myself, "how can anyone feel sadness when there is so much joy in the world, so much to experience, so much to give, and so much to love."

Just before my 40th birthday, I went to a Teepee a friend owed and fasted for three days. I sang and journaled and danced in preparation for my party. 77 people came to celebrate with me. I looked and felt like I was 29. People made prayer bundles for me with sage and wise words. It was a beautiful ceremony.

I read a book soon after that had an impact on me, titled Goddesses in Every Woman, by Jean Shinoda Bolen. She wrote about the seven primary goddesses, and that as women, we were whole and holy if we could embrace the gifts and the learnings from each one. I realized that I had devoted myself mostly to Aphrodite, the goddess of love, and Artemis, the goddess of healing who is focused and independent. I wanted to embrace Demeter, the mother Goddess and Hera, the goddess of marriage.

My whole life had been given to service, even when I was a child, being the eldest girl of 8 children. My father left us 2 weeks after my littlest sister was born. I was 14 and determined to create a good life for my family, both monetarily, and in making sure that my little brothers and sisters had the best care possible, ranging from potty training to making birthday cakes. My mother was suicidal, understandable after just giving birth, having 8 children, no education, and no husband. We had no money, and ate potato soup for months. I remember that first Christmas. I was determined that everyone would have one gift that they would love, even though there was no money. I took a bus to downtown Denver and decided that I would steal presents for everyone. I loved the dress that I stole for my little sister Kelly who was 6 months old. It was pink and lacey and the most beautiful dress I had ever seen. I wanted her to have it. I was ferocious and determined and probably that was why I never was caught. I made sure that each person in our family had something they would love. I never stole again. And my "sin" felt totally worth it on Christmas morning, seeing the surprise and delight on everyone's faces as they opened their gift from "Santa".

I wanted to experience the fullness of womanhood. I wanted to claim a life that was mine. The spiritual community that I was devoted to went through an upheaval. My spiritual mentor died. The base of my service and love was deeply challenged. I wanted a relationship. I wanted to have a child. I went through some sort of mental breakdown. I could not get out of bed, or return calls. I went on anti-depressants and could only handle that for six weeks. I hated the numbness it made me feel. I would see little children and break into tears. I felt my life had gone by and I was childless and alone. I had always loved children and felt that there was a child spirit that had been surrounding me for years wanting to come through me.

I finally pulled myself together and decided to go to graduate school. Part of my training was an internship in another city. I told my new friends there that I was open for a relationship and a child. A friend introduced me to Bert. I was not physically attracted to him, as he was shorter than me and bald. But he had charisma. He was creative and playful and sensual, and he wanted a child so I went for it.

The first 6 months were magical. He cooked delicious food for me. He would tell people he was in love with a woman in her 40's that had a body of a 25-year-old. We made magical love every night we were together. He would draw a bath and line the perimeter with candles. When I graduated, he gave me 250 roses. Women would stop me on the street and would say "it must be wonderful to be loved by Bert!" I was smitten, I had never been treated so lavishly by anyone. We had a deep relationship physically, emotionally, and creatively.

If it feels too good to be true, it isn't. Little by little, things started to show up that I had never experienced in my relationships. First were the lies that he squirreled away as not true or my imagination. Then were the rageful episodes where he would explode and yell at me and others. I had never been around anger like that and I would start shaking and be short of breath. Then there was the retelling of stories, events that happened with his friends or with me that simply were not true. Then it moved to the physical. We were going to a friend's house for sushi and he exploded and grabbed my arms and would not let me out of the car. This verbal and sometimes physical abuse continued. One time he pulled a chair out from under me and I crashed unto the floor and he said it just slipped. Another time he started thrashing out at me in the car and we narrowly avoided a crash.

I thought our love could save us, the typical mistake. If there was such deep love, then couldn't we work through this? I wanted him to take a mens' course, he did, and it seemed to only increase his anger. We took a meditation class together, and that didn't solve anything. We went to couples counseling together. The counselor loved him. In session, he would go very deep to a level of understanding that would bring tears to her eyes. He understood, he was cooperative and loving and willing. Less than 5 minutes outside of the session he would start yelling and be verbally abusive all over again.

It was a confusing time for me. I had "fallen" for him, and would say that the highs were awesome highs, and the lows were the worst thing I had ever experienced. People told me I just was afraid of commitment since I hadn't ever committed to anyone. I loved our experience, and I hated the anger and the effect it was having on me.

I finally decided to leave after 6 months and told him I was. It turned into a physical altercation where I ended up with bruises, and bloody scratches on my neck and hands. The police were called, he went to jail and there was a restraining order against him. About 4 weeks later, I opened my door to an odd smell. My shoes were outside my house. There was human shit in them. My neighbors had seen his craziness and were sure Bert did this. I thought it was a prankster as I lived near the college. I could not fathom that he would do such a thing to me. Even with this sick evidence, I was in denial. If only I had pressed this issue with the police. This decision would later come back to haunt me as surely as if I told a judge about this and had evidence my life would have turned out differently.

12 weeks after the breakup, I discovered I was pregnant. I wondered if I should tell him. I was emotional and hormonal and decided to rely on a sign that might indicate I should. This was a huge mistake. My "sign" was seeing him in Denver at a trade show which was a place neither of us had ever been to before. I decided to break the restraining order and tell him about the pregnancy. He was overjoyed, and said he wanted to take care of the baby and me. I thought mistakenly, that having a child between us would stop the craziness. I thought my child would be better off with the two of us together. It only made it worse. My friends did an intervention and got me away from him. He admitted during this time of attempted reconciliation that he had put his shit in my shoes while there was a restraining order in place. He did it very carefully he said, and was gleeful about it.

I was 45, unemployed, fresh out of graduate school, pregnant for the first time with no money, and yet overjoyed at being pregnant. And I was totally scared about doing this by myself. I would sing to my belly, and journal and tell this little soul that I would be there for him no matter what.

During the ensuing years, this is a synopsis of the abuse:
- Bert would call me at 3 in the morning, yell and hang up
- He returned Raphael after parenting time with a huge dog bite on his eye lid. His face was like a balloon. He blamed it on Raphael and not the dog. I tried verbally and legally to ban the dog from all visits and failed.
- He would send emails and faxes and leave messages that were verbally abusive and angry

- I had to hire attorneys as Bert repeatedly tried to take Raphael from me which cost me over $89,000.
- He would create vicious lies and stories about me which he used to try and turn Raphael against me. He would lie in court and tell these convincing stories to judges, friends and even the mayor of Denver.
- He always put his needs ahead of his son so everything was at his convenience.
- Bert finally abused his own son who ended their relationship at age 16. The abuse precipitated a psychotic break, he was hospitalized, medicated, depressed and from then on had trouble scholastically. He stopped playing sports, and started smoking. Bert still pressed the courts for parenting time and blamed me of course for turning his son against him! Thankfully with treatment, love, time and patience, Raphael is doing much better. He has always been an old soul and wise beyond his years. He is compassionate, kind, a great listener and a stellar human being.

Please please please, if there is even a hint at abuse, get the hell out of the situation. You can't change anyone, only yourself, so don't pretend that if you just love him enough, or if he "loves" your child, that things will change for the better, they won't. Look at the signs of narcissistic personality disorder which is rarely treatable. A narcissist will go to great lengths to win you over and then try to destroy you. The game is getting you to believe so much in their awesomeness that you can't imagine they would be anything but that.

These are the personality traits of a narcissist:
1. has a grandiose sense of self-importance (e.g., exaggerates achievements and talents, expects to be recognized as superior without commensurate achievements)
2. is preoccupied with fantasies of unlimited success, power, brilliance, beauty, or ideal love

3. believes that he or she is "special" and unique and can only be understood by, or should associate with, other special or high-status people (or institutions)
4. requires excessive admiration
5. has a sense of entitlement, i.e., unreasonable expectations of especially favorable treatment, demanding compliance with his or her expectations
6. is interpersonally exploitative, i.e., takes advantage of others to achieve his or her own ends
7. lacks empathy: is unwilling to recognize or identify with the feelings and needs of others
8. is often envious of others or believes that others are envious of him or her
9. shows arrogant, haughty behaviors or attitudes

I feel I allowed him to rob my soul. Part of it was naivete. Part of it was so wanting a child and a partner after all of these years. Part of it was feeling that I had slipped from God's grace. I spent 19 years trying to protect myself and my son and it took a huge toll on my spirit, my finances and my life.

Today I am partially healed. I have a good life. I am married. I love where I live. I assist women entrepreneurs in creating personal, professional and global transformation. I have two pets that I adore. I love my son and as has often been said, to the moon and back! It's been a rough ride, and I have learned so much. This is only a partial story of all that happened, and I hope in writing this chapter it will assist other women to listen deeply to their intuition and not be blinded by "love". Please have the courage to leave the second you experience abuse. Your soul is worth so much more.

Chapter 30

Kaelen Revense

"I believe that YOU are your greatest gift AND your greatest adventure!"

~ Kaelen Revense

From the ages of 5-8 years old, I was sexually abused by one of my male cousins. I always wondered why he wanted to have just me and him sleep outside in our camper when we would visit their family. And then one night while we were sleeping in the camper I woke up to find he was doing things to me that I did not understand and yet at the same time it felt nice but I knew it was wrong.

When I became completely awake, I ran into my aunt's home and told my parents and his parents that he had pulled down my underwear. That was all I could say because I did not know what else to call it! I felt so ashamed and guilty for what had happened and from that moment on, I have not had a good relationship with my cousin. This experience really colored the way I looked at men and once I got married, I realized that emotionally and mentally, it affected me in being a wife and mother.

Where are you now on your healing path?

In this moment in life, I am now a Career Wellness Coach helping women discover they are their greatest gift and their greatest adventure so they can take back their power, discover their magnificence, fall in hard core love with who they truly are, all the way down to the cellulite on their backsides, so they can share those gifts they have uncovered with their loved ones and ultimately the world if they chose!

I have gone through and continue to go through personal development courses to improve me and love me even more! I absolutely LOVE being Kaelen Marie Revense and am so grateful for ALL of my pain, trials, challenges, depression, weight gains and losses and gains again, anxiety, and the way I had inflicted myself with body hating and body bullying because each one of these experiences has created the person I am today!

They are all MY GIFTS and mine alone! I have opened them to reveal the greatest person I could never have imagined without them! I am still on my healing journey because other experiences happen in life that I need to heal from. So today I choose to look at them as gifts I am privileged to open so I can receive my very best self!

What has been the most positive thing you have done for yourself to overcome the trauma of your past?

One of the most positive things I have done for myself to heal from this was when a dear friend of mine who's children had been molested by her father-in-law, encouraged me to face my cousin, tell him how I was feeling, forgive him so I could move on in life.

With her by my side, I went to his office over 20 years ago and told him how what he had done to me really hurt and caused so much pain, that I was in a place I wanted to forgive him so I could move on with my life. My friend told to be prepared if he did not apologize as most abusers blame their victims. She was right, he did not apologize but I know that day when I left his office, I finally felt release and freedom from over 25 years of pain. From then on, I have continued to work on my own self improvement by hiring coaches and becoming the best person I can possibly be by loving me completely!

What words of wisdom can you offer to those who have just begun their own journey of healing?

Trust, trust, trust your inner voice!!!

As women we are blessed with "women's intuition" and it is a REAL GIFT!!! We are inherently closer to the Divine because of our ability to co-create and bear children.

As a result, we are given this beautiful inner voice that warns us of danger, when things just aren't right, that we need to proceed with caution. One of my coaches told me that the day I am able to completely listen and trust that inner voice of intuition is the day I will live in my greatest power!

What resources can you recommend to those just beginning on their journey of healing?

Find a coach (not a therapist) because you want to heal from the inside out, not the outside in! I actually have a male coach who stands in his truth as a virtuous man, full of integrity, love and honor! It may be a woman coach that works best for you, but it does not matter what their gender is, only as long as they are the BEST FIT FOR YOU!!! And your inner voice will tell you this!

Find your inner voice; learn to listen to it, and then TRUST IT!!!

Founder of: The Gifted Formula Blueprint: **www.KaelenRevense.com**

Chapter 31

Jane M. Powers

Stand Up! Speak Up! Find Your Truth! Command Your Inner Power

~Jane Powers

Many little girls' bedtime routines include kissing and hugging mom and dad goodnight, singing a lullaby, or snuggling up with a favorite story book. Not mine. Bedtime for me included laying in anticipation of the beginning of my routine. With the flip of a switch, the hallway light streamed into my room and onto my bed. As I looked toward the doorway, the ever-familiar silhouette made his appearance. I learned early on there was no escaping the fate of what was about to happen next…and for the following 14 years.

My story began before I ever had words to express what was happening in my life. I, as many, lived in a world of dark secrets held deep inside. Sexual abuse weaved its way through many generations in my family. My abuse goes back as far as I can remember, with my earliest memory being put down for a nap in my crib and latest memory being my freshman year of high school.

Growing up, I did my best to be the average kid. I smiled a lot to hide the shame and lies. I became quite adept at playing the role of the student, athlete, helper, and best friend. My life was like a play and I was the lead. I knew how to live out the family secret. My world was a lonely one. I was alone in my silence with no one to tell and no one to save me. Each night, I prayed for someone to put a stop to the constant sexual abuse being inflicted by my father and brother(s). Each night, my prayers went unanswered.

Based on the evidence in my life, the only logical conclusion I came to was that God forgot about me. I could not imagine that God would allow the horrible events in my life to happen to any child. The way I saw it, if God remembered me, there would be no way my suffering would have lasted so long or at all, for that matter. I was destined to break out of my silence and free the reticent scream buried deep inside of me.

Breaking the silence as a survivor, I learned that having a voice was a matter of life or death. The key to my healing has been finding my voice and telling my truth.

My journey to tell the truth began in 1983 when I was a junior in college. Every day I felt there was something wrong with me. Happiness eluded me and I was continuously angry. One day, I was in my dorm room feeling the usual, "What is wrong with me?" thoughts. My anger grew to the point where I put my fist through my plate glass window. That was the day I knew I needed help. I began my extremely long journey into therapy. I am sure many of you know this lengthy journey well; funding your therapists' cars and homes by spending more money trying to undo what was done to begin with.

I entered therapy with no memories, only feelings of shame, guilt, and anger. I soon discovered the power of the mind. Many of us are able to survive any degree of trauma because our mind wipes out memories all together. Thinking I was going to heal the affects of alcoholism, I attended a role-playing workshop that acted out my family interactions. That was the day that changed my life. Instead, a flood of memories raced through my mind like a movie. I had been sexually abused! There was no way it could be true, none of my sisters talked about it, no one did! We were an upper middle class family living in the country club. We looked great from the outside. It could not be true. Since I grew up being told I had an amazing imagination, of course I believed I imagined it all.

One of the hardest steps in my process was, believing my own memories. Many survivors doubt their memories are real. Think about it…it's tough to believe that our own family members or loved ones could do that to us. AND if they did, what did that say about us?

I dedicated myself to working on my healing beginning that day in 1983 and have not stopped since. I was on the Oprah Winfrey show breaking my code of silence in the episode announcing everyone in the studio audience had lived through the tragedy of sexual abuse. I have spoken to thousands and counseled many to help them stop the cycle of their sexual abuse. My ultimate mission in life is to help people find their voice.

Our voice is what brings us to life. It helps us find and live in our power. It took me many years to find my voice. I can share my story with you but, like many, it is not a pretty one. It tells a tale of a family of seven each living their own pain of survival in one form or another. I can tell you about my mother's alcoholism and her tragic death when I was 14 years old. I can share with you the constant shaming and humiliation in my childhood. I can tell you my story, of which many of you have the same. But what I truly want to share is how to LIVE. My goal is to bestow upon you that you are more than what happened to you. You are not who they made you to believe you are. You are here to speak YOUR truth.

I don't know about you but years of therapy taught me one thing: I did not have to relive my past in order to have a future. I went into therapy, rolled up my sleeves, and dove into incredibly tragic and painful memories, thinking I had to go through the ultimate pain to live the ultimate joy. Instead, it was like putting salt on the wound. I would come out sweaty and rung out, thinking: "Now that was a good session!" It took me years to understand that it's about our relationship to the story and accompanying feelings, not the actual incidents themselves.

How does one relate differently to the story? My hope is to help you to find your voice and open yourself up to a new way of living in not just survivorship, but thrivership.

Speak UP!

There is no greater power than finding your voice! I don't mean go out and tell the world you were sexually abused, although I do not suggest anyone hide it. I encourage you to begin with a simple "yes" or "no". It can be a simple, "No, I don't want liver and onions" OR "Yes, I would love pizza" (I mean who wouldn't). I love the saying, "make your yes be yes and your no be no, no lukewarm". "NO" was not something we even dreamt of saying to our abusers. At the age of seven, I tried to say no to my father. Trust me when I say I never did that again.

If we can begin to find our voice in everyday things, we begin to free the dark secrets that keep us in shame and guilt. One of the key issues with unreleased truths is that it becomes our new normal. We keep secrets so long that we often don't realize we do it. Unfortunately, it leads to a variety of issues on physical, emotional, mental, and spiritual levels.

There are so many hidden side effects of sexual abuse that most are unaware of it in their lives. The key to unlocking those hidden side effects is your voice. So, begin speaking up and decide what you would love.

Stand UP!

As children of abuse, we were put into a system of dysfunction and trained to behave within that system. In my family, I was taught on day one that you had no choice and no voice. You could not express your opinion or dissatisfaction about anything, let alone your disgust about what was happening to you. As a result, many learned to become invisible, not wanting to stand out or take a stance about anything. The best solution to abuse is to stand up for yourself and never take a back seat to anyone. It makes me crazy when I see people discounting their own opinion or conceding to others, so they don't make waves. I say, stir it up, make waves, and be heard and respected for your truth.

Find your Truth!

Our truth is, many times, based on the limiting stories or paradigms we believed growing up. The trick is to tell a different truth or story. It is so simple but not at all easy. For years, I believed I was "the kid who";

you name it I believed it. I was the kid who was never going to make it because of what happened to me or what was said about me. I bought into someone else's truth.

How do we go from someone else's truth to knowing our own truth?

The first step in finding your truth is to realize the story you believe to be true about yourself and/or what story do you tell about yourself? You want to start putting everything into perspective and become aware of what you believe about yourself. Make a list of the statements you make about yourself.

It might sound like this:
"I'm not smart enough."
"I am too fat, too short, too old."
"I am not worthy."

Now write the exact opposite of those statements and gather evidence to prove they are true.

For example, if you believe you are not smart enough, prove why you are. I thought that about myself, told a new story, and found evidence to support my new belief. I graduated with a 4.0 from college and passed 2 real estate tests in record time. Also, despite my past, I created two multi- million-dollar businesses and built a 6-figure coaching business. I help people speak with confidence and sell with authority, to ultimately find their voice. What is your proof?

Find your proof, truth and live it!

Command your Power!
As a thriver, I had to find my power and learn how to command it each day. I was afraid to stand out and be found out that I was a fraud. I was the kid who....! My identity was established the minute I began my training for "victimhood". I was forced to relinquish my innocence and power for someone else's gain. I was used to satisfy my family member's desire and exertion of power. As a result, I like many, progressed through

life feeling mad, sad, guilty, shameful, dirty, and like there was something wrong with me. Unexpressed feelings are visible in everything we do and they take away our power. They appear, consciously or unconsciously, in our relationships (intimate or not), successes, careers, kids, authority figures, and more, if we do NOT command our power.

The best and only way, in my opinion, to command your power is to give every feeling and thought a voice. If we "stuff" or try and eliminate these feelings, they will spill out somewhere. We must give ourselves permission to get out what needs to be expressed.

Here are a few tips to help:

1. Scripting: This is an exercise that allows you to talk to you. You simply write out the conversation as if you are writing script for a play. In this example, if I feel sad, I put down the initials, SJ, for Sad Jane. I start the script with J for Jane like this....

   J: So, SJ would you share why you are sad?
   SJ: I am really sad but can't tell anyone about it.
   J: If you could tell someone what would it sound like?
   SJ: Response...

2. Post-its: One of my favorite ways to identify my power is by owning the various traits of my personality. I have The Doubter, The Critic, The 5 year old and a few more traits that like to express themselves each day. Trust me, when I started this type of work, I thought I was crazy. I have discovered it is the best way to know who I am and what my triggers are in various situations. Take a few post-it notes and name the various traits or parts of yourself.

3. Good ole' fashion journaling: There is nothing like writing in your journal. I actually hated journaling. It was boring and took too long but it is incredibly effective.

Early in my process, I asked myself, "Why Me?" each day I was going through my healing. Today, I say, "Who better than me?" I didn't go through what I went through to be a victim or a survivor. I lived through my version of tragedy to make a difference in the world. I am solid in my knowledge that I am here to help people. Help people who have lived through sexual abuse be more than what happened to them. Sexual abuse and the damage it causes can leave us with deep-seated beliefs we may not even be aware of. Every day I continue to see the effects of my abuse but I work very diligently to own the effects and not let the effects own me.

My journey was not easy, nor is it ever over. I am a thriver and the only way I keep that "status" is to be aware. I must Speak Up, Stand Up, Find my Truth, and Command my Power. In absence of these values and commitments, I am a victim to my past. No matter the stage of healing you are at, decide to step up on top of the piles of stories, beliefs, and abuse and BE FREE!

Jane's Video Interview: **https://youtu.be/g2Z5y56E4uM**

Website: **www.Janempowers.com**

Chapter 32

Favorite Quotes

"I Do Not Owe My Past a Place in My Future"

"Don't let the darkness from your past block the light of joy in your present. What happened is done. Stop giving time to things which no longer exist, when there is so much joy to be found here and now."

~Karen Salmasohn

✦

"Given the dark pains I've experienced, nothing is more generous and loving than the willingness to embrace grief in order to forgive."

✦

"Loving myself is the most important thing I could ever do for myself."

✦

"The irony is that we attempt to disown our difficult stories to appear more whole or more acceptable. But our wholeness, even our wholeheartedness actually depends on the integration of all of our experiences, including the falls."

~Brené Brown

✦

"She couldn't feel her wings, but she knew they were there. So she built a ladder to the sky, and when she touched the clouds, she would remember how to fly."

~Atticus

✦

"I used to extinguish by the weight of living, but some days, indeed in brief moments, I was able to reach into myself, dust off my courage and ask myself, "Where's my fire?""

~ (adapted from a quote by D. Foy)

✦

"The inability to forgive is as painful as the wound itself."

~Caroline Myss

✦

"In order to benefit fully from the healing power of telling your story, you must resist from holding anything back. It is time to strip off the mask, forget what everyone else will think or say and tell it like it is without apology."

✦

"We do not choose to be born. We do not choose our parent, or the country of our birth. We do not, (most of us), choose to die; nor do we choose the conditions of our death. But within the realm of choicelessness, we do choose how we live."

~Joseph Epstein

✦

Inside us, there is something greater than what we know. We just need to release it.

~ Marianne Williamson

✦

"Faith is like wi-fi…it is invisible, but it has the power to connect you to what you need."

~ author unknown

✦

The same boiling water that softens potatoes hardens eggs.

~ author unknown

✦

"When you're in the middle of a story, it isn't a story at all, but only a confusion; a dark roaring, a blindness, a wreckage of broken glass and splintered wood; like a house in a whirlwind, or else a boat crushed by the icebergs or swept over the rapids, and all aboard powerless to stop it. It's only afterwards that it becomes anything like a story at all. When you are telling it, to yourself or someone else."

~ Margaret Atwood

✦

"There is no greater threat to the critics and cynics and fear mongers than those of us who are willing to fall, because we have learned how to rise."

~ Brené Brown

✦

"It certainly takes more courage and strength to walk away from a bad situation than to stay in it. Staying is familiar, no matter how bad it is, you kind of know what you are up against. Walking away is stepping into the unknown and uncharted waters."

~ Becky Norwood

✦

"Character is formed by the willingness to accept responsibility for one's own life, it is the source from where self respect springs."

~Joan Didion

✦

"Our deepest fear is not that we are inadequate. Our deepest fear is that we are powerful beyond measure. It is our light, not our darkness that most frightens us.

✦

We ask ourselves, 'Who am I to be brilliant, gorgeous, talented, fabulous?' Actually, who are you not to be? You are a child of God. Your playing small does not serve the world. There is nothing enlightened about shrinking so that other people won't feel insecure around you.

✦

We are all meant to shine, as children do. We were born to make manifest the glory of God that is within us.

✦

It's not just in some of us; it's in everyone. And as we let our own light shine, we unconsciously give other people permission to do the same. As we are liberated from our own fear, our presence automatically liberates others."

~Marianne Williamson

✦

Forgiveness, even of myself, does not change the past, but it makes the future infinitely brighter!

~ author unknown

✦

"Forgiveness, quite frankly, is the most selfish thing you can do. Because it is the greatest thing you can do for yourself."

~Caroline Myss

✦

"Nobody knew she carried a secret universe in her heart, but those brave enough to enter that space and see what a beautiful galaxy her love could be."

~Mark Anthony

✦

"Healing comes from gathering wisdom from past actions and letting go of the pain that the education cost you."

~Caroline Myss

✦

"Do not speak badly of yourself, for the warrior
that is inside you hears your words and is lessened by them.
You are strong and you are brave. There is a nobility
of spirit within you. Let it grow."

~David Gemmell

✦

"Courage is taking the first steps to your dream even when
you can't see the path ahead."

~Becky Norwood

✦

"You gain strength, courage, and confidence by every
experience in which you really stop to look fear in the face.
You are able to say to yourself, 'I lived through this horror. I
can take the next thing that comes along.'"

~Eleanore Roosevelt

✦

Stand Up! Speak Up! Find Your Truth!
Command Your Inner Power

~Jane Powers

✦

"I am in the world to change the world."

~Kathe Kollwitz (1867-1945)

✦

"Stars can't shine without darkness."

~D.H. Sidebottom

✦

I wish you a happy life! It's your time to Dream it.
Plan it. Live it!

✦

Enjoy the Adventure!

~Traci Bogan

✦

"One thing that was told to me when I began this journey
was that being a survivor was sort of like a club. Becoming a
member was a horrible ordeal, but you will never find a group
of more understanding and loving people who don't judge
and will help you heal in whatever way they can."

~Karin Tyson

✦

"Create the highest, grandest vision possible for your life,
because you become what you believe."

~Oprah Winfrey

✦

"Be kind whenever possible; it is always possible."

~Dalai Lama

"Even though you may want to move forward in your life,
you may have one foot on the brakes. In order to be free, we
must learn how to let go. Release the hurt. Release the fear.
Refuse to entertain your old pain. The energy it takes to hang
onto the past is holding you back from a new life. What is it
you would let go of today?"

~ Mary Manin Morrissey

✦

"Try to be a rainbow in someone's cloud."

~Maya Angelo

✦

"We come to love not by finding the perfect person, but by learning to see an imperfect person perfectly."

~Sam Keen

✦

"Three things cannot be long hidden:
the sun, the moon, and the truth."

~Buddha

"Love is my gift to the world. I fill myself with love,
and I sent that love out into the world."

~Dr. Wayne Dyer

✦

"There is no force more powerful than
a woman determined to rise."

~Mantra Yoga Mag

✦

"It is what it is. Move forward or stay behind. Your choice."

~Brenda Hammon

✦

"Becoming a Victim is not a choice. Becoming a survivor is."

~Juan Quotes

✦

"Everything happens for a reason."

~ Diana Dunham

✦

"Tread Lightly."

~Carmel de Bertaut

✦

"I could never be truly happy unless I was putting myself first. And to put myself first, I needed to start speaking the truth."

~Katie Devine

✦

"I do not believe I came from the school of hard knocks. Instead I believe I am from the school of the most fortunate. I have been incredibly lucky to survive my past and have gone on to live a productive and fulfilling life. Thank heavens for the kind and generous people who guided me, helped and showed me that life can be amazing when you surround yourself with loving and caring friends and family."

~Shannon O'Leary

✦

"One reason people resist change is because the focus on what they have to give up, instead of what they have to gain."

~author unknown

✦

"It is never too late to be who you were meant to be."

~Karen Sprecher

✦

"Peace is not the absence of conflict,
but the ability to cope with it."

~Robert Fulghum

✦

"Ignorance is not bliss, Ignorance is dangerous. Knowledge is
bliss and powerful. Be bliss, be powerful!"

~Tessa Milne

✦

"If you're broken, you fill yourself with broken people."

~Iyanla Vanzant

"If you don't ask, you don't get."

~Roberta Brown

✦

"I believe that YOU are your greatest gift AND
your greatest adventure!"

~ Kaelen Revense

✦

"There is nothing more beautiful and powerful than the
courage of a woman."

~ Teresa Syms

✦

"Scars remind us where we have been, they don't define
where we are going."

~David Rossi

✦

"What will you do with this one wonderful,
wild and precious life?"

~Mary Oliver

✦

"Never say Never!"

~Sondra Joyce

✦

"Whenever two or more of you are gathered
in harmony and joy, magic happens!"

~Sondra Joyce

✦

"I do this to be a voice, to speak for those who can't speak."

~ Matt Sandusky

✦

Chapter 33

Resources

Darkness to Light: Darkness to Light has a vision of a world where childhood abuse does not exist because they know that prevention is possible. When adults take their *Stewards of Children*® child sexual abuse prevention training, they commit to protecting children. And when that happens, children can lead happy, healthy lives, safe from sexual abuse. **http://bit.ly/2j9aWuA**

R.A.I.N.N. has helped 2.4 Million people since 1994. RAINN'S Mission (Rape, Abuse & Incest National Network) is the nation's largest anti-sexual violence organization. They operate the National Sexual Hotline: 800.656.Hope in partnership with more than 1,000 local sexual assault service providers across the country and operates the DoD Safe Helpline for the Department of Defense. RAINN also carries out programs to prevent sexual violence, help victims, and ensure that perpetrators are brought to justice.**Online.rainn.org and rain.org/es https://www.rainn.org/**

http://www.peacefulheartsfoundation.org/

http://littlewarriors.ca/

https://www.planusa.org/because-i-am-a-girl

http://plancanada.ca/because-i-am-a-girl

American Foundation for Suicide Prevention (AFSP)
https://www.afsp.org/ Call **1.800.273.TALK (8255)**
if you or someone you love is experiencing thoughts of suicide.
Understanding and preventing suicide through research,
education and advocacy.

www.ingramcontent.com/pod-product-compliance
Lightning Source LLC
Chambersburg PA
CBHW052003090426
42741CB00008B/1526